THE CHARTERED INSTITUTE OF MARKETING

Chartered Postgraduate Diploma in Marketing
ASSESSMENT WORKBOOK

Valid for assessments up to September 2013

The Chartered
Institute of Marketing

BPP
LEARNING MEDIA

First edition November 2012

ISBN 9781 4453 9155 7

e-ISBN 9781 4453 9626 2

British Library Cataloguing-in-Publication Data
A catalogue record for this book
is available from the British Library

Published by

BPP Learning Media Ltd
Aldine House, Aldine Place
142-144 Uxbridge Road
London W12 8AA

www.bpp.com/learningmedia

Printed in the United Kingdom by

Polestar Wheatons
Hennock Road
Marsh Barton
Exeter, EX2 8RP

Your learning materials, published by BPP Learning
Media Ltd, are printed on paper obtained from
traceable sustainable sources.

We are grateful to The Chartered Institute of Marketing for
permission to reproduce in this workbook the syllabus,
tutor's guidance notes and past examination questions.

Contents

The Chartered
Institute of Marketing

1 Aim of the Assessment Workbook

This Assessment Workbook has been designed to help you prepare for assessments relevant to the Chartered Postgraduate Diploma in Marketing qualification. This Workbook does not aim to teach you the content that you need to know in order to pass – content is covered in the corresponding Study Texts.

The aim of the Assessment Workbook is to provide you with strategies that will help you succeed in your assessment.

To do this we:

- Give CIM-specific advice in terms of what is expected of students
- Provide hints and tips based on our understanding of CIM examiner requirements
- Give suggested solutions to the sample exams and recent real exams
- Use the sample assignments to provide advice using example answers based on hypothetical cases

2 The Chartered Postgraduate Diploma syllabus

The Chartered Postgraduate Diploma in Marketing is aimed at Brand Managers, Strategic Marketing Managers, Business Development Managers and middle to senior Marketing Managers.

If you are a graduate, you will be expected to have covered a minimum of half your credits in marketing subjects.

You are expected at this level of the qualification to demonstrate the ability to manage marketing resources and contribute to business decisions from a marketing perspective.

The aim of the qualification is to provide the knowledge and skills for you to develop an 'ability to do' in relation to strategic marketing planning and leading its implementation. CIM qualifications concentrate on applied marketing within real work-places.

The complete Chartered Postgraduate qualification is split into two stages. Stage 1 comprises four units. Stage 2 is a work-based project that should enable those who pass it, with the relevant experience and continuing professional development, to become Chartered Marketers.

The four units that comprise the Stage 1 qualification are:

- Unit 1 Emerging Themes
- Unit 2 Analysis and Decision
- Unit 3 Marketing Leadership and Planning
- Unit 4 Managing Corporate Reputation

The syllabus for Units 2, 3 and 4, as provided by CIM, can be found in each of the corresponding unit chapters of this Assessment Workbook.

Unit 1, Emerging Themes, is not covered in this Workbook. For this unit we have produced a Study Support Text, a standalone product that includes the content and guidance required to succeed in this unique unit.

3 A note on pronouns

On occasions in this Assessment Workbook, 'he' is used for 'he or she', 'him' for 'him or her' and so forth. While we try to avoid this practice it is sometimes necessary for reasons of style. No prejudice or stereotyping according to gender is intended or assumed.

4 Additional resources

CIM's supplementary reading list and other resources

CIM requires you to demonstrate your ability to 'read widely'. To help you achieve this, CIM issue an extensive reading list for each unit. Within our Study Texts we identify what we believe to be essential reading.

Throughout the Study Texts and Assessment Workbook we also refer to other **resources produced by CIM** including examiner reports, sample assessments and past assessment questions. These provide valuable insight into what the examiner requires you to do. You should visit the CIM website regularly to check what resources are available.

Remember, as a professional you should **read widely** (online and offline), and ensure you keep up-to-date with current marketing issues.

BPP Learning Media Study Materials

There are a number of study products available to help you succeed in the Chartered Postgraduate Diploma in Marketing including Study Texts, this Assessment Workbook and a set of Passcards.

We produce **Study Texts** and **Workbooks** for three units (Unit 2 Analysis and Decision, Unit 3 Marketing Leadership and Planning and Unit 4 Managing Corporate Reputation). We also produce a **Study Support Text** for Unit 1 Emerging Themes.

The Texts highlight and explain the key concepts you need to learn. They also contain practical activities and real-world examples to keep you engaged and reinforce your understanding.

Whether you read them from cover to cover, or use them more as a reference tool, BPP Learning Media's Chartered Postgraduate Diploma Study Texts will ensure you have access to the knowledge you need to succeed.

This **Chartered Postgraduate Diploma Assessment Workbook** covers units 2, 3 and 4 of the Chartered Postgraduate Diploma. It includes tips on tackling assessments, insights from examiners, and practical examples to ensure you're well prepared.

BPP Learning Media also produce a handy set of spiral bound **Passcards**. These A6-sized revision cards reinforce key topics and help consolidate your learning. They provide an excellent recap of key points.

Additional online resources for students and tutors from BPP Learning Media

BPP Learning Media plan to produce additional resources to support students and tutors.

Please check the web address www.bpp.com/lm/cimresources for further details.

CHAPTER 1

An overview of CIM Chartered Postgraduate Diploma assessments

Topic list

1 What is the Institute looking for in students?

There are a few key points to remember as you study and prepare for your CIM assessment with regard to the Institute's expectations of you. To put this into context, try to remember the following:

(a)   You are studying for a **professional** qualification. This means that you are required to use professional language and adopt a business approach in your work. Ten percent of the available marks are awarded for the 'format and presentation' of your work.

(b)   You are expected to show that you have read widely. Make sure that you read the quality press and read *Marketing*, *The Marketer*, *Research* and *Marketing Week*. Adding real-life examples into your work helps to show that, not only have you read widely, but you are illustrating the points you are making in a convincing way.

One way to improve your knowledge is to make full use of CIM's online *Knowledge Hub*. Your student membership entitles you to full access to this goldmine of both academic and non-academic press. The *Knowledge Hub* is an access point to lots of good sources in order to answer the specific assignment question posed. Also on the CIM's website, you will find a *Shape the Agenda* section. This is another good source, which enables you to show you are familiar with current CIM research programmes. Within the 'Shape the Agenda' pages you will find highly relevant and recent papers on current topics of importance to the CIM. New agenda papers are published every six months. In recent years, topics have included market segmentation, managing marketing, marketing metrics, relationship building communications, and social marketing.

(c) Take note of the marketing initiatives you come across on a daily basis.. TV commercials are a good reflection of the current marketing thinking in the company concerned. Consider the messages, channel choice and timings of ads. It is surprising how much you will learn! This will help you build a portfolio of real life marketing examples to use in your assessment work.

(d) You will already be familiar with the way the Institute writes the exam papers and assignments. CIM uses a specific approach, which is referred to as 'The Magic Formula', to ensure consistency when designing assessment materials. Make sure you are fully aware of the requirements for this level, as it will help you interpret what the examiner is looking for (a full description of the Magic Formula appears later in this section).

(e) Make certain that you use Harvard referencing correctly. This is explained later in this section and is important to master because it is a key requirement of the CIM that you use it (mostly in assignments). You should not need reminding that direct quotes from a textbook, research paper, news report or article should all be clearly cited. The rule is: read, learn and inwardly digest and afterwards: write in your own words. Just changing a word here and there (paraphrasing) is, after all, a form of plagiarism!

CIM requires you to use Harvard referencing for a number of reasons. Firstly, they need to ensure that your assignment is your own and an original piece of work. Plagiarising someone else's work is a serious offence and if you were found to be copying from someone else or another source, such as a textbook, then you would fail. It is for this reason that the Institute requires assignments to be presented as both paper and electronic versions so that they can run your work through anti-plagiarism software.

The second reason for insisting on Harvard referencing is to demonstrate that you have read widely around the syllabus. It is important that you use a variety of sources in your assignments to justify and back up your ideas. If, in exams - although you are not expected to include references- you can at least remember and add the names of key authors and sources, then it adds more depth to your answers.

(f) Ensure that you read very carefully all assessment details sent to you from the Institute. CIM is very strict with regard to deadlines, completing the correct paperwork to accompany any assignment or project and making sure that you have your CIM membership card with you at the exam. Failing to meet any assessment entry deadlines or failure to complete written work on time will mean that you will have to wait for the next round of assessment dates and will need to pay the relevant assessment fees again.

Please note: This workbook deals with only three of the four units of the Chartered Postgraduate Diploma (Stage One). All four units have a need for the inclusion of contemporary issues, but *Emerging Themes,* even more than the other three. That is the reason that BPP has produced a separate text for Emerging Themes, published as a **Study Support Text.**

1.1 Required skills at the Chartered Postgraduate Diploma level

The Institute has also identified key skills that you are expected to develop throughout your studies. With this qualification, you are moving to a new level in your career possibilities. The Chartered Postgraduate Diploma is not an end in itself, but a doorway to professional progress. Once you have qualified, it is expected that you will move into a much more strategic role in your chosen field. By virtue of your studies here, your capabilities should be enhanced.

The Chartered Institute of Marketing

You should be able to:

- Think strategically (understanding competitive positioning and developing business strategy)

- Think creatively, communicate effectively and understand Integrated Marketing Communications (IMC)

- Make strategic decisions (taking strategic responsibility for marketing decisions and understanding the broad organisational impact of them, as well as guiding corporate decisions)

- Undertake cultural design and redesign

- Lead and influence others

- Manage growth/transition and transformation

- Be a catalyst for unlocking human potential

- Formulate strategic plans (by developing vision and long-term direction and managing corporate resources effectively, including developing proficiency at budget planning)

As well as improving your performance at the more tactical level of:

- Evaluating and prioritising activities
- Preparing contingency plans
- Being able to balance options, competing interests and needs
- Managing the head-count and the human capital and be proficient at coaching and mentoring
- Developing internal and external networking

The intention is to ensure that CIM's Chartered Postgraduate Diploma will be a move towards establishing successful students as *'professional practitioners'* in the field of marketing, who can contribute to an organisation's success.

1.2 'Postgraduateness'

The CPGD is a postgraduate/Master's level qualification and, at this level, it is assumed that candidates already have a comprehensive background in marketing. Certainly the requirement for studying for this Diploma is a business or marketing degree, where half of the credits come from marketing AND a range of senior marketing management experience. Nevertheless, Senior Examiner reports that are posted to the Learning Zone website (http://www.cimlearningzone.co.uk) often state that candidates lack 'postgraduateness' and this means that you will need to do rather more than simply demonstrate knowledge and apply that knowledge to a range of business contexts.

At postgraduate level, candidates need to be able to assess the relevance of different theories and concepts for a particular business situation and justify why they would, or would not, recommend their use as a basis for current practice, or indeed as the rationale for changing business practice. This ability requires candidates to engage with a range of concepts and theories, evaluate them for their suitability (critical analysis) and then develop a rationale for why they are appropriate. Senior Examiner Assessment Review Report (Managing Corporate Reputation), March 2012.

1.3 Command words

Command words are very important at all levels of CIM's qualifications. Command words pop up in all assessments and have very specific meanings, with which you should be familiar. The following is a selection of command words and their meaning, at this level.

Appraise: meaning evaluate, judge or assess. Here, you should be able to provide evidence of a depth of understanding and a substantial body of knowledge working with ideas and models that are at the forefront of the discipline. You should be able to demonstrate awareness of the implications of conflicting ethical dilemmas.

Argue: Provide reasoned arguments for, or against, the issue and arrive at an appropriate conclusion. Specifically, you should be able to critically analyse complex, incomplete or contradictory areas of knowledge of a strategic nature and communicate the outcomes effectively.

Assess: Evaluate or judge the importance of something, referring to appropriate schools of thought. Specifically, to be able to assess a wide range of theoretical principles/methodologies, applicable to the discipline and your own work and apply these within a senior marketing management context.

Compare and contrast: To look for similarities and differences leading to an informed conclusion. To be able to synthesise and analyse the similarities and differences between two or more contexts, in a manner that is innovative and original.

Define: Write the precise meaning of a word or phrase. Quote a source if possible. To be able to define key words reflective of a body of knowledge at level 7 and can show that the distinctions contained or implied in the definition are necessary or desirable.

Describe: Give a detailed account of something. To be able to critically analyse complex, incomplete or contradictory ideas and information and to present the findings clearly and effectively.

Demonstrate: Explain, using examples. To be able to explain and utilise theories and concepts from the forefront of the discipline/practice demonstrating a mature and analytical understanding and awareness of principles and practice at a strategic level.

Discuss: Investigate or examine by argument and debate, giving reasons for and against. To be able to synthesise information, with critical awareness, in a manner that is innovative and original, using language appropriate for a senior level.

Explain: Make plain, interpret and account for, enlighten, give reasons. To be able to present complex, incomplete or contradictory areas of knowledge of a strategic nature and communicate the information effectively.

Illustrate: Give examples to make clear and explicit, to demonstrate something. To be able to apply relevant contemporary issues, demonstrating a mature and analytical understanding and awareness d of strategic issues that are at the forefront of the discipline.

Justify: Support recommendations, explanations or arguments, with valid reasons for and against the issue. To be able to articulate complex arguments with critical awareness in a manner which is innovative and original.

Outline: Give main features or general principles, ignoring minor details. To be able to selectively identify valid and relevant information from a range of sources relevant to level 7.

Recommend: Put forward proposals, supported with a clear rationale. To be able to produce reliable, valid and incisive conclusions and proposals based on complex, incomplete or contradictory data or information, appropriately contextualised to a given context.

State: Present in a clear brief form. To be able to present complex, incomplete or contradictory data or information in a clear and concise manner, appropriately contextualised to a given context.

Summarise: Give a concise account of the key points, omit details and examples. To be able to summarise complex, contradictory or contentious information in a logical and concise manner.

Critically analyse: Means the examination of a topic, together with thoughts and judgements about it. Specifically at this level, you should be able to analyse complex, incomplete or contradictory areas of knowledge and diverging schools of thought using appropriate models, principles and definitions.

Critically evaluate: Means to make an appraisal of the value (or not) of something, its validity, reliability, applicability. Specifically, to be able to critically evaluate complex, unpredictable and contentious information, often in a specialist context and arrive at informed conclusions and argue alternative approaches.

Please note: these two last are, arguably, the most important at this level.

2 CIM's Magic Formula

The Magic Formula is a tool used by the Institute to help both examiners in writing exam and assignment questions and you to more easily interpret what you are being asked to write about. It is useful for helping you to check that you are using an appropriate balance between theory and practice for your particular level of qualification. There is a danger that is inherent to all models and formulae: you will want to use this in too prescriptive a fashion. Avoid this pitfall!

Contrary to the title, there is nothing mystical about the Magic Formula and simply by knowing it (or even mentioning it in an assessment) will not automatically secure a pass. What it does do, however, is to help you to check that you are presenting your answers in an appropriate format, including enough marketing theory and applying it to a real marketing context or issue. After passing the Professional Diploma in Marketing, and as you continue to study for this higher level CIM qualifications, you will be expected to evaluate more and apply a more demanding range of marketing decisions. As such, the Magic Formula is weighted with an even greater emphasis on evaluation and application as you move to the Postgraduate CIM I.

Graphically, the Magic Formula for the Chartered Postgraduate Diploma in Marketing is shown below:

Figure 1.1   The Magic Formula for the Chartered Postgraduate Diploma in Marketing

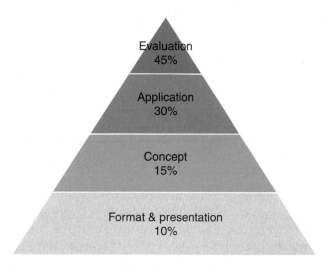

You can see from the pyramid that, for the Chartered Postgraduate Diploma, marks are awarded in the following proportions:

- **Format and Presentation – 10%**

    You should remember that you are expected to present your work professionally, which means that for assignments it should **always** be typed and attention should be paid to making it look as visually appealing as possible, even in an exam situation. It also means that the Institute will stipulate the format that you should present your work in. The assessment formats you will be given will be varied and can include things like reports to write, slides to prepare, emails, memos, formal letters, press releases, discussion documents, briefing papers, agendas, and newsletters.

- **Concept – 15%**

    Concept refers to your ability to state, recall and describe marketing theory. The definition of marketing is a core CIM syllabus topic. If we take this as an example, you would be expected to recognise, recall, and write this definition to a word-perfect standard to gain the full marks for concept. Understanding marketing concepts is clearly the main area where marks will be given within your assessment.

- **Application – 30%**

  Application based marks are given for your ability to apply marketing theories to real life marketing situations. For example, you may be asked to discuss the definition of marketing and how it is applied within your own organisation. With this sort of question 30% of the marks would have been awarded as the 'concept' aspect of the Magic Formula. You will gain the rest of the marks through your ability to evaluate to what extent the concept is applied within your own organisation. Here, you are not only using the definition but are applying it in order to consider the market orientation of the company.

- **Evaluation – 45%**

  Evaluation is the ability to assess the value or worth of something through careful consideration of related advantages and disadvantages, or weighing up of alternatives. Results from your evaluation should enable you to discuss the importance of an issue, using evidence to support your opinions.

  Using the example of whether or not your organisation adopts a marketing approach, you could be asked to 'evaluate' this. It would then be expected that you would provide reasons and specific examples why you thought they might take this approach and also to consider the reasons why marketing orientation is not fully achieved, before coming to a final conclusion.

  Note: The way grading criteria for this level links to the Magic Formula, at this level, is described in Appendix 2 (at the back of this book).

3 Revising for your exam

3.1 Revision for the exam

Unit Two (Analysis & Decision) is the only one at this level assessed by exam.

Evaluation is the largest component at this Postgraduate level of Study. When it comes to actually revising, there are some essential strategies.

Firstly, revision should not be left to the last minute – it really starts the moment that you study a topic and complete your reading. Once you have completed the required topics, you should make sure that you fully understand the implications to a range of different contexts. Now is the time to start collecting examples of marketing practice by making notes of observations you have made through your own work and on relevant articles you have read within the business and marketing press. The work done earlier will prove invaluable when you get to your final stage of revision.

Practise, practise, practise – this is key to passing CIM exams. Throughout your course you should have been completing past exam papers. Attempt the questions in this workbook along with the additional practise topics given You should also check your learning by completing the quick quizzes in the study texts.

3.2 Key steps in revision

The run-up to the exam is a very important time. You must remember the following three main points, which we will then break down into more detailed advice.

Point 1: Use your time sensibly

1. Be honest with yourself about **how much study time you have**. Remember that you must **eat, sleep,** and of course, **relax.**

2. **How will you split that available time between each subject**? What are your weaker subjects? They will need more time.

 The Chartered Institute of Marketing

3   **What is your learning style**? Know yourself and adapt your study time accordingly.

4   Are you taking regular breaks? Most people absorb more if they do not attempt to study for long uninterrupted periods of time.

Do you have quality study time? Unplug the phone. Let everybody know that you're studying and shouldn't be disturbed.

Point 2: Set yourself realistic goals

1   Have you set a clearly defined objective for each study period?
2   Is the objective achievable?
3   Will you stick to your plan? Will you make up for any lost time?
4   Are you rewarding yourself for your hard work?
5   Are you leading a healthy lifestyle?

Point 3: Believe in yourself

Are you cultivating the right attitude of mind? There is absolutely no reason why you should not pass this exam if you adopt the correct approach.

- **Be confident** – you've passed exams before, you can pass them again
- **Be calm** – plenty of adrenaline, but no panicking
- **Be focused** – commit yourself to passing the exam

3.3 Scrapbook technique

When it comes to starting final revision, one of the most useful exercises you could do before the exam is to carry out what we like to call the 'scrapbooking activity'. This will help you to remember the key theories but also to prepare a bank of good marketing examples that may be easier to remember once you get into the exam room. To complete the activity you will need:

- A large piece of paper or a flipchart
- Some coloured pens
- Newspapers, marketing magazines, blog examples, and so on

Step 1   **Outline theories (list, mind maps, diagrams)**

Aim to create one sheet per topic for the module you are revising. For example, when you are revising for the *Analysis and Decision* exam, you may have a sheet for the topic 'stakeholder analysis'. This is where you will need to think about how you like to remember information so, for example, do you remember visually or do you list items in your mind; do you like diagrams, or prefer pictures to words? If you are not sure, then think about how you might direct somebody to your house. Would you be more likely to write a list of directions, draw a detailed map or a more basic diagram? The important point is that there are many books which tell you how to create mind maps or similar memory aides, but at this stage you will not have time to master those and you need to be spending your time actually revising. Therefore, go with whatever works best for you, and get everything that you can think of about individual topics down on that piece of paper. Be creative with your colours if you wish. For instance, you may find it easier to colour code different subtopics.

Step 2   **Review your outline and add more detail**

At this stage, you should go back to your notes and texts and add in more detail, especially in terms of adding little bits of information about the good and bad points, advantages and

disadvantages and contexts in which activities may be more or less appropriate. Now, complete this process for all the topics on the modules syllabus.

Step 3 **Adding examples**

Move onto the example creation stage. Pull together as many copies of news reports, marketing press and business journals as you can from the last year. You will need scissors and some glue. By now, you have probably guessed what you will be doing. Go through and stick as many examples as you can find about each of the topics onto your relevant sheets.

The result

By the time you have finished, you should have a huge bank, not only of the key theories and topics, but some good examples to add depth to your answers.

Once you reach the final stages of your exam revision, you will need to be at the point where you are checking that you remember enough for your time in the exam room. It is here that you will want to be completing whole mock exams to check that you have written in enough depth. You should also be testing yourself to see if you remember key theories and can commit them to memory. You would find BPP Learning Media's Passcards useful in this respect. Here, the sort of information you have included in your own flipchart scrapbook will have been reduced down to hand-sized cards, which you could use for a last minute memory jog. You may find it useful to write key words to trigger your scrapbooked marketing examples at the bottom of the relevant Passcard page.

4 Writing assignments and work-based projects

The Assignment based units offer you considerable scope to produce work that provides existing and future **employers** with **evidence** of your **ability.** It offers you a **portfolio** of evidence which demonstrates your abilities and your willingness to develop continually your knowledge and skills. It will also, ultimately, help you frame your continuing professional development in the future.

The units in which you are required to submit an assignment are:

Unit 1 – Emerging Themes (This unit is NOT dealt with here, because an entirely new, all-inclusive *Study Support Text,* **prepared by the Senior CIM Examiner and Deputy, is available separately)**

Unit 3 – Marketing Leadership and Planning

Unit 4 – Managing Corporate Reputation

It does not matter what type of organisation you are from, large or small, you will find substantial benefit in the work-based assignment approach to assessments. In previous years, some CIM Chartered Postgraduate Diploma students could choose between exam and assignment routes to their qualification. There were several cases where students made their own organisation central to their assessment and produced work to support their organisation's activities, resulting in subsequent recognition and promotion: a success story for this approach! This is a key reason why the Institute and employers worked together to develop the 2009 syllabus with a large proportion of the final qualification being assessed in this way. The CIM wanted to develop a syllabus that would train marketers to move directly into a strategic marketing role and perform effectively from day one.

So, using your own organisation can be beneficial (especially if your employer sponsors you). However, it is equally valid to use a different organisation, as long as you are familiar enough with it to base your assignments on it. This is particularly useful if you are between jobs, taking time out, returning to employment or studying at university or college.

The Chartered
Institute of Marketing

4.1 Structure and process

The **assignments** that you will undertake during your studies are normally set **by CIM centrally** and not by the study centre. All assignments are validated to ensure a structured, consistent approach. This standardised approach to assessment enables external organisations to interpret the results on a consistent basis.

The purpose of each assignment is to enable you to demonstrate your ability to research, analyse and solve problems in a range of different situations. You will be expected to approach your assignment work from a professional marketer's perspective, addressing the assignment brief directly and undertaking the tasks required. Each assignment will relate directly to the syllabus module and will be assessed against that content.

All of the assignments clearly indicate the links with the syllabus and the assignment weighting (ie, the contribution each task makes to your overall marks). You will also be given information regarding the assessment criteria (we will cover this more fully later).

Once your assignments have been completed, they will be marked by the Examiners of the Institute. After that, your grade will be forwarded to you by CIM in the form of an examination result.

4.2 Preparing for assignments: general guide

The whole purpose of this guide is to assist you in presenting your assessment professionally, both in terms of presentation skills and overall content. The Magic Formula shows that 10% of the available marks are awarded for format and presentation. It will therefore be helpful to consider how best to present your assignment. Here, you should consider issues of detail, protocol and the range of communications that could be called upon within the assignment.

4.2.1 Presentation of the assignment

You should always ensure that keep electronic copies of your assignment. Occasionally, assignments go missing, or second copies are required by CIM. The CIM also requires you **to submit an electronic copy**, which may be scanned through anti-plagiarism software. You should save your assignment using the following convention for the title:

Centre name-Unit title (abbreviated eg, MIR/SM)-session-CIM student registration number

Example: BPP-DCVTM-Dec2012-12345678

You should also ensure that:

- Each assignment should be clearly marked with your study centre, your CIM student registration number and, at the end of the assignment, a word count. **Do not under any circumstances put your name on the assignment because the CIM may not accept it**. You cannot use fancy folders to present your work and it should be fastened with a treasury tag in the top left hand corner. You will need to complete and attach a copy of CIM's 'Assignment Front Sheet and Declaration Form' otherwise, your work will not be accepted.

- The assignment presentation format should directly meet the requirements of the assignment brief (reports and presentations are the most commonly requested communication formats). You **must** ensure that your assignment does not appear to be an extended essay. If it does, you will lose marks.

- A word or page limit will be included in the assignment brief. These are specified by CIM and must be adhered to. Students whose word count is above or below 10% of the required risk their work failing. The word count does not include headings, references, bibliography, appendices or tables. Font size 11 must be used throughout, except in the case of the tables that can present font size 8. Tables will however be counted if they are thought to constitute most or all of your assignment. When slides are

presented, any word count will apply to the accompanying notes and not the slides. The word count is required at the end of your document.

- Appendices should clearly link to the assignment and can be attached as supporting documentation at the end of the report. However, failure to reference the appendices by number (eg Appendix 1) within the report is a key problem. Only use an appendix if it is essential and clearly adds value to the overall assignment and remember that you cannot gain marks directly for items in the appendix. The appendix should never act as a "waste bin" for all the materials you have come across in your research, or a way of making your assignment seem somewhat heavier and more impressive than it is.

4.3 Time management for assignments

One of the biggest challenges we all seem to face day-to-day is that of managing time. When studying, that challenge seems to grow increasingly difficult, requiring a balance between work, home, family, social life and study life. Therefore it is of the utmost importance to your success for you to plan wisely the limited amount of time you have available.

Step 1   **Find out how much time you have**

Ensure that you are fully aware of how long your module lasts and the final deadline. If you are studying a module from September to December, it is likely that you will have only 10–12 weeks in which to complete your assignments. This means that you will be preparing assignment work continuously throughout the course.

Step 2   **Plan your time**

Work backwards from the final deadline and submission dates, and schedule your work around the possible time lines. Clearly if you have only 10–12 weeks available to complete three assignments, you will need to allocate a block of hours in the final stages of the module to ensure that all of your assignments are in on time. This will be critical, as all assignments will be sent to CIM by a set date. Late submissions will not be accepted and no extensions will be awarded. Students who do not submit will be treated as a 'no show' and will have to resubmit for the next period and undertake an alternative assignment.

Step 3   **Set priorities**

You should set priorities on a daily and weekly basis (not just for study, but for your life). There is no doubt that this mode of study needs commitment (and some sacrifices in the short term). When your achievements are recognised by colleagues, peers, friends and family, it will all feel worthwhile.

Step 4   **Analyse activities and allocate time to them**

Consider the **range** of activities that you will need to undertake in order to complete the assignment and the **time** each might take. Remember, too, there will be a delay in asking for information and receiving it.

Always add in time to spare, to deal with the unexpected. This may reduce the pressure that you are faced with in meeting significant deadlines.

Warning!

The same principles apply to a student having 30 weeks to do the work. However, a word of warning is needed. Do not fall into the trap of leaving all of your work to the last minute. If you miss out important information or fail to reflect upon your work adequately or successfully, you will be penalised for both. Therefore, time management is important whatever the duration of the course.

 The Chartered Institute of Marketing

4.4 Tips for writing assignments

Everybody has a personal style, flair and tone when it comes to writing. However, no matter what your approach, you must ensure your assignment meets the **requirements of the brief** and so is comprehensible, coherent and cohesive in approach.

Think of preparing an assignment as preparing for an examination. Ultimately, the work you are undertaking results in an examination grade. Successful achievement of all four modules in a level results in a qualification.

There are a number of positive steps that you can undertake in order to ensure that you make the best of your assignment presentation in order to maximise the marks available.

Step 1   **Work to the brief**

Ensure that you identify exactly what the assignment asks you to do.

- If it asks you to be a marketing manager, then immediately assume that role.
- If it asks you to prepare a report, then present a report, not an essay or a letter.
- Furthermore, if it asks for 5,000 words, do not then present 1,000 or 7,000.

Identify whether the assignment should be **informal or formal (almost certainly the latter),** to whom it should be **addressed**, its **overall purpose** and its **potential use** and outcome. Understanding this will ensure that your assignment meets fully the requirements of the brief and addresses the key issues included within it.

It would be a good idea at this point to check your understanding of the assignment with your tutor. Studying with a CIM centre means that you should expect a minimum **one hour** of one-to-one tuition time specifically with the assignment in mind.

Step 2   **Address the tasks and pay attention to the Assessment Criteria**

It is of pivotal importance that you address **each** of the tasks within the assignment. **Many students fail to do this** and often overlook one of the tasks or indeed part of the tasks.

The Assessment Criteria that the CIM will use to assign marks is clearly shown on the assignment briefs. Make sure that you look at the criteria and think about whether you have fully addressed them. Likewise, make it easier for your examiner to identify where you are attempting to meet the criteria by, wherever possible, using similar terms for individual sections of your assignment.

Step 3   **Information search**

Many students fail to realise the importance of collecting information to **support** and **underpin** their assignment work. However, it is vital that you demonstrate to the CIM your ability to **establish information needs**, obtain **relevant information** and **utilise it sensibly** in order to arrive at appropriate decisions.

You should establish the nature of the information required, follow up possible sources, time involved in obtaining the information, gaps in information and the need for information.

Consider these factors very carefully. CIM are very keen that students are **seen** to collect information, **expand** their mind and consider the **breadth** and **depth** of the situation. In your *Personal Development Portfolio* (for your CPD hours), you have the opportunity to complete a **Resource Log**, to illustrate how you have expanded your knowledge to aid your personal development. You can record your additional reading and research in that log, and show how it has helped you with your portfolio and assignment work.

Step 4   Develop an assignment plan

Your **assignment** needs to be structured and coherent, addressing the brief and presenting the facts as required by the tasks. The only way you can successfully achieve this is by **planning the structure** of your assignment in advance.

Earlier on in this unit, we looked at identifying your tasks and working backwards from the release date in order to manage time successfully. The structure and coherence of your assignment needs to be planned in a similar way.

When planning the assignment, you should include **all the relevant information as requested** and you should also plan for the use of models, diagrams and appendices, where necessary.

Your plan should cover your:

- Introduction
- Content
- Main body of the assignment
- Summary
- Conclusions and recommendations where appropriate

Step 5   Prepare draft assignment

It is always good practice to produce a **first draft** of an assignment. You should use it to ensure that you have met the aims and objectives, assignment brief and tasks related to the actual assignment. A draft document provides you with scope for improvements, and enables you to check for accuracy, spelling, punctuation and use of English.

Use the '**week in a drawer**' trick, which involves completing your first draft and then not looking at it for at least a week. When you return to the draft, areas where you were not entirely clear will now be very apparent to you. **Your study centre tutor is only allowed by the CIM to give feedback on your written work once.** It would therefore be advisable to make the most of this opportunity once you have reflected on areas of improvement after this week.

Step 6   Prepare Final Document

In the section headed 'Presentation of the Assignment' in this unit, there are a number of components that should always be in place at the beginning of the assignment documentation, including **labelling** of the assignment, **word counts**, **appendices** numbering and presentation method. Ensure that you **adhere to the guidelines presented**, or alternatively those suggested by your Study Centre.

4.4.1 Writing reports

Students often ask 'what do they mean by a report?' or 'what should the report format include?'

There are a number of approaches to reports, formal or informal: some report formats are company-specific and designed for internal use, rather than external reporting.

For Continuous Assessment process, you should stay with traditional formats.

Below is a suggested layout of a Report Document that might assist you when presenting your assignments.

- *Title Page* includes the title of the report, the author of the report and the receiver of the report.

- *Acknowledgements* – this should highlight any help, support, or external information received and any extraordinary co-operation of individuals or organisations.

- *Contents page* – provides a clearly structured pathway of the contents of the report – page by page.

 The Chartered Institute of Marketing

- *Executive summary* – a brief insight into purpose, nature and outcome of the report, in order that the outcome of the report can be quickly established.

- *Main body of the report divided into sections, which are clearly labelled*. Suggested labelling would be on a numbered basis eg:

    - 1.0 Introduction
    - 1.1 Situation Analysis
    - 1.1.1 External Analysis
    - 1.1.2 Internal Analysis

- *Conclusions* – draw the report to a conclusion, highlighting key points of importance, that will affect any recommendations that might be made.

- *Recommendations* – clearly outline potential options and then recommendations. Where appropriate justify recommendations in order to substantiate your decision.

- *Appendices* – ensure that you only use appendices that add value to the report. Ensure that they are numbered and referenced on a numbered basis within the text. If you are not going to reference it within the text, then it should not be there.

- *References/Bibliography* – whilst in a business environment a bibliography might not be necessary, for an **assignment-based report it is vital**. It provides an indication of the level of research, reading and collecting of relevant information that has taken place in order to fulfil the requirements of the assignment task. Where possible, and where relevant, you could provide academic references within the text, which should of course then provide the basis of your bibliography or list of references. A list of references is often preferable to a bibliography because it is more obvious that you have actually used the sources you have stated (see *A brief guide to Harvard referencing* in the Appendix).

5 Writing a company background

One item often required within the appendix to accompany your assignments is a background of your organisation or company.

Even if you think that you may have covered this previously it may be worth adding it to the appendix. CIM examiners have said on many occasions that candidates frequently struggle to write clear and concise company backgrounds.

Firstly, it is useful to think about why you are being asked to provide this background. Imagine for a moment that you are an examiner faced with a few hundred scripts. Each candidate is likely to refer to a different company or division, the large majority of which will be unknown to the examiner. Unless the examiner is directly familiar with the company you are referring to, it is quite possible that they may take your responses out of context or misinterpret your meaning because they do not know the specifics or nature of your organisation. Think about when you first move to a new job. To begin, it is difficult to see how the bigger organisational picture fits together because you may not know much about the industry, the culture of the organisation and key factors of influence. The same situation is true for the examiner, so the purpose of your company background is to provide a brief induction document into these issues.

Two points need to be remembered:

1   The examiner may use your company background to put the rest of your answer into context.
2   Your background should be clear, concise (no longer than two pages of A4) and well structured.

5.1 What should be included in the company background?

The following can be used as a checklist to ensure that you have included sufficient detail without rambling.

The organisation

- Organisation's name, including a parent company or more recognised brand.

- Type in terms of size, sector, ownership and legal structure.

- When established and major events in the organisation's history.

- Growth and broad strategic aims.

- Mission statement.

- Broadly outline any other details specific to the organisation which are important to the assignment tasks eg, culture, staff, structure, supply chain partners of importance.

The market

- Market overview and the organisation's position within the market, eg, market leader
- Approximate size of the market
- Key competitors
- Customer groups and their characteristics
- Broad key trends eg, a rapidly growing market

Product/service range

- Description of the product/service range
- Key feature, associated benefits and unique selling proposition
- Historical developments of the product/service range
- Details of complementary products
- Details of substitutes

You are likely to find that not all of these points are relevant to your organisation but it will be useful at least to run through them in order to think about the key implications that will help put your company into an appropriate context for the examiner. Frequently when we work within organisations much of the knowledge we possess is unconscious. You may find it helps to show your final company background to someone who is not familiar with yours. Ask them to read your background and then in their own words to describe your organisation back to you – you will find this helps you to see whether you have produced a realistic impression.

At the Chartered Postgraduate Diploma level, you may not be specifically asked for a company overview, but, for the reasons given, we recommend that you do add one as an appendix item.

5.2 An example company background

Example company background (Appendix 1)

The following overview, for the purposes of demonstration, is based loosely on a real-life organisation, but the case study organisation and its situation are essentially fictional.

Appendix 1: Organisation overview

The Wetland protection society

The Wetland Protection Society (WPS) is a leading UK conservation organisation, dedicated to preserving wetland ecosystems and habitats for the benefit of wildlife and human communities around the UK.

Background

Wetlands are areas of land saturated with moisture, providing a safe and supportive ecosystem for many different species of plants, fish, birds and insects. They perform useful functions in regulating local environments, but are also valuable as places for human recreational and educational activities such as wildlife observation, fishing, camping and field research.

By 1993, half the world's wetlands had been drained for development, or flooded for use as recreational lakes (*New Scientist,* 1994). Since the 1970s, there has been a drive to preserve wetlands for their natural and educational functions.

Foundation and legal form

The WPS was founded in 1953 by a prominent ornithologist and nature writer, Sir Douglas Brown OBE. It was incorporated as a not-for-profit company limited by guarantee (with members acting as guarantors, rather than shareholders). It is defined as a voluntary organisation, set up for charitable purposes ('the advancement of environmental protection or improvement', as defined by the *Charities Act 2006*), and is registered as a charity in England, Wales and Scotland.

The Society has over 100,000 members, and enjoys the patronage of HRH The Prince of Wales.

Aims and activities

The core aims of the Society are: to conserve wetlands and wetland species; to raise awareness of the issues that affect their survival; and to enhance people's lives through opportunities to learn about, be close to and collaborate in the protection of Nature.

The key activities of the Society, in pursuit of these aims, include:

- *Wetland reserve management*. The Society manages six wetland reserves, with visitor centres enabling public access to designated areas, while restricting access to vulnerable areas. Together, these reserves cover some 1,500 hectares of wetland, receiving almost one million visitors per year. Some of the sites are designated as Special Protection Areas (under the EU directive on the Conservation of Wild Birds) or listed areas under the Convention on Wetlands of International Importance (Ramsar Convention, 1971).

- *Education*. The Society seeks to change public perception and foster public support for wetlands. Educational programs include guided tours for the general public, school visits, media liaison, visitor/information centres and information for Society members.

- *Research and environmental consultancy*. The Society conducts and publishes scientific research to enable conservation and planning bodies to understand and address the threats faced by wetland areas. Its consultancy division (WPS Consulting) is often contracted by corporations and government bodies to assess the impact of development plans and to recommend strategies for impact minimisation: all profits raised through the Consultancy are gifted back to the Society to support its conservation work.

- *Lobbying and influence*. The focus of lobbying is to secure protected status for key wetland areas and endangered species, and to oppose harmful development (eg, the construction of dams) in sensitive areas.

- *Fundraising*. In support of all the above activities, the Society raises funds via means such as: annual membership subscriptions (offering a range of member benefits, including free entry to WPS wetland centres and a free quarterly magazine); corporate membership and sponsorship; public donation appeals; events (including the annual Water Life Day volunteer fundraising day); government research and conservation grants; and commercial activities (such as consulting and merchandise sales).

In recent years, there have been increasing requests for the Society to participate in conservation ventures, lobbying campaigns and research programmes in overseas countries.

The UK charity sector

Each year, the British public gives nearly £5 billion to over 170,000 charities (Peck *et al,* 2004). According to the Charities Aid Foundation (CAF, 1996), the charitable categories that benefit most from voluntary donations in the UK include: health (eg, Cancer Research), general welfare (eg, the Salvation Army), international aid (eg, Red Cross), heritage and environment (eg, National Trust) and animal protection (eg, RSPCA).

The WPS sees itself firmly in the heritage and environment category, but is often perceived as an animal protection charity. Environmental and wildlife charities tend to be supported by a younger and less well-off donor population than the national average (CAF, op cit), but also tend to have a good success rate in attracting corporate sponsorship, due to their positive and CSR-related associations.

Charities compete with each other for funds, and the charities that the WPS regards as its closest direct competitors are the Royal Society for the Protection of Birds (RSPB), the National Trust and the World Wide Fund for Nature (the top three conservation charities by voluntary income, [CAF, *op cit*]) as well as other conservation and wildlife charities. There is a positive level of co-operation between charities within this sector, however: major charities collaborate on lobbying and research funding, and even co-operate on marketing (eg, holding bi-monthly meetings to co-ordinate their timetables of events and appeals).

Organisation structure

The Society employs a core of around 120 permanent staff, as well as volunteers (eg, as centre guides) and contractors (eg, on research projects and event management). The permanent management structure of the Society can be summarised as follows.

Figure 1.2   Organisation structure

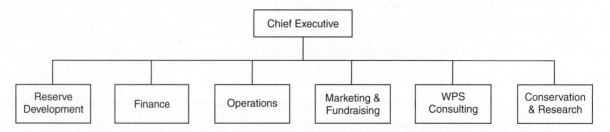

In addition, the Society has a Council, responsible for the general control and management of the charity, comprising a Chair, Treasurer and a number of other distinguished naturalists and academics.

▶ **Assessment tip**

A few things to notice about our specimen overview:

- It occupies a maximum of two A4 pages.

- It gives a fairly broad overview, but focuses in more detail on some areas. You might decide to include a survey of organisation culture, key suppliers/distributors/allies, business processes, future plans and so on. Be selective in the information you include.

- It covers the details required by the project brief, but not in a formulaic way: 'aims and activities' replaces 'products/services', for example, and 'the charity sector' replaces 'target market'. Be flexible in your thinking, and remember to contextualise your material to the particular organisation you are looking at.

- It deliberately includes elements which will support later discussion of relationship marketing (the theme of the project): mentioning a range of stakeholder audiences, the potential for an international element, fundraising and lobbying.

- It references sources of information (which would be cited in the References appendix of the report).

This task is worth doing well. Although it earns no marks, it may be the first thing the assessor reads, and therefore needs to create a good first impression of your clarity, judgement and professionalism.

Don't neglect the wealth of support material available on the CIM website (www.cim.co.uk), and the video tutorials, recorded webinars, white papers and other reports available on the Learning Zone (www.cimlearningzone.co.uk). Members can log in and enjoy fast online access to marketing journals, magazines, books and reports.

The range of resources available include: a collection of databases from Ebsco covering journals, newspapers, company profiles and country reports, a range of online books from MyiLibrary – such as Drayton Bird's amazing *Commonsense direct and digital marketing* and a collection of marketing journals from Emerald.

You can also access Marketing ExpertBeta, where you can find templates, legal guidance and all sorts of useful information

Whatever your specialist field, there is likely to be a market research report in CIM's library to stimulate your thinking.

CHAPTER 2

Analysis and decision

Topic list

1 Unit overview and syllabus

This unit consists of three parts: **Strategic audit**, **Strategic options**, and **Making strategic marketing decisions**. The overall purpose of the unit is to prepare students to undertake a strategic audit of an organisation, assess its capability and capacity to deliver the organisation's business and marketing strategy in a challenging, dynamic and diverse global market place, and to recommend a strategic option, or decision, based on a full critical evaluation of the various options available.

To achieve this aim, students will be expected to carry out the following:

- First they will undertake a sophisticated strategic audit which will help to prioritise the key issues, opportunities and risks facing an organisation in meeting its future objectives. This will be based on a clear and detailed assessment of an organisation and its performance, and the issues and challenges it faces in creating and delivering best value.

- They will use their strategic audit of an organisation to generate strategic options and critically evaluate those options in respect of the key issues faced by the organisation.

- Finally, after exploring the wide range of strategic options available to an organisation to meet its corporate and business strategy, students will need to recommend an option based on, and justified by, a critical evaluation of its suitability in the specific situation.

In doing the above, students should be able to undertake both qualitative and quantitative analysis of the relevant options and be able to make strategic marketing decisions based upon such analysis, justifying decisions and providing reasoned arguments for their recommendations. They will be expected to apply a range of financial and risk models to support their assessments and demonstrate an understanding of how the decisions will support the achievement of the organisation's vision, mission and strategic business and marketing objectives.

Overarching learning outcomes

By the end of this unit, students should be able to:

- Undertake a strategic marketing audit, assessing an organisation's competencies, competitive advantage, market performance, customers, competitors, product and service portfolios, positioning, value proposition and market impact

- Assess the impact of external factors on an organisation and its strategic intent and direction

- Utilise the strategic marketing audit to critically evaluate a range of strategic marketing options available to an organisation, including innovation, mergers, acquisitions, partnering, alliances, environmental sustainability and CSR, in order to deliver best value growth and expansion opportunities for the organisation

- Utilise a range of financial and other measurement tools to assess the financial and non-financial benefits of recommended strategic marketing decisions

- Utilise a range of risk assessment tools to critically assess the risk of strategic market decisions and their impact upon an organisation, including financial, corporate and reputational risk.

Part 1 – The strategic audit (all parts have equal weighting)

1.1 – The strategic marketing audit (weighting 35% of this part)

1.1.1	Utilise a range of techniques, processes and market information to assess the external marketing environment including: ▪ The competitive environment ▪ Customers ▪ Channels (local, international and global) ▪ Market structures
1.1.2	Utilise market-based information to critically evaluate an organisation's strategic position within the market place, including consideration of specific positioning issues: ▪ Competitive positioning ▪ Competitive advantage ▪ Value creation ▪ Competitor analysis

 The Chartered Institute of Marketing

1.1.3	Utilise a range of tools to critically evaluate an organisation's ability to understand its current customer base and their buying behaviour, in order to be able to develop customer insight and meet their preferences:
	■ Value proposition
	■ Segmental analysis and consumer profiling
	■ Strategic account analysis
	■ Consumer profiling
1.1.4	Assess the potential for strategic uncertainty in the external market and the extent to which it involves trends or events, and show how it will impact upon an organisation:
	■ Scenario construction
	■ Market sensing
	■ Forecasting techniques to assess the potential and probability that trends or events will occur
	■ Forecasting techniques utilised to assess timeline for trends and events arising and their impact
	■ Assessing market stability and attractiveness

1.2 – The strategic marketing audit: internal (weighting 35% of this part)

1.2.1	Utilise a range of models and techniques to undertake a strategic audit of the internal environment:
	■ Resource and competency audit (physical, human and intangibles)
	■ Portfolio analysis
	■ Value chain and resource utilisation
	■ Innovation audit
	■ Cost efficiency
	■ Product life-cycle
	■ Organisation's vision, mission and values
	■ Degree of customer and market orientation
	■ Comparative and best practice analysis
	■ Core competencies
	■ Organisational culture
	■ Financial performance
1.2.2	Critically evaluate the resource-based view of an organisation and the value of this approach in developing resource and capability to deliver an organisation's vision and mission:
	■ Resources, capabilities and competencies
	■ The elements of resource-based competitive advantage
	■ Knowledge as a resource
1.2.3	Critically evaluate the fit between an organisation's culture and its current strategy, and assess its ability to be flexible and agile in a changing marketing environment:
	■ Environmental influences on organisational culture
	■ Mintzberg's organisational structures
	■ Handy's cultural styles
1.2.4	Utilise a range of internal information and assessment tools to evaluate an organisation's strengths and weaknesses in order to assess its readiness for development, including an assessment of:
	■ Competencies, assets and culture
	■ Value chain and value proposition
	■ The state of the organisation's financial and non-financial assets

1.3 – Developing the organisation's strategic intent and direction
(weighting 30% of this part)

1.3.1	Critically evaluate an organisation's current strategic intent, based upon its vision, mission, values and stakeholder expectations:
	■ Organisational purpose, mission and values
	■ Defining organisational focus
	■ Stakeholders analysis
	■ Relationship portfolios
	■ Organisational configuration
	■ CSR and ethics
1.3.2	Critically analyse the role of strategic intent in shaping an organisation's strategy development:
	■ Strategic intent and strategic vision
	■ Strategic intent and leadership
	■ Intent and flexibility
	■ Strategic opportunism versus strategic drift

Part 2 – Strategic options

2.1 – Assessing strategic marketing decisions (weighting 20% of this part)

2.1.1	Critically evaluate the determinants of strategic options and choices:
	■ Past and current strategies
	■ Organisational capabilities and constraints (financial and non-financial)
	■ Financial capabilities and constraints
	■ Organisational strengths and weaknesses
	■ Product-market opportunities
	■ Sources of competitive advantage (Porter)
	■ Warfare analogies in strategy (Kotler)
2.1.2	Critically evaluate how strategic options can be developed to reflect an organisation's:
	■ Value proposition
	■ Assets and competencies
	■ Business function strategies
	■ Functional strategies and programmes
	■ Competitive advantage
	■ Sustainability

2.2 – Strategic options available to a growing organisation (weighting 80% of this part)

2.2.1	Critically evaluate the nature of innovation and new product development (NPD) in marketing and the related factors impacting upon marketing decisions, including ongoing innovation management within an organisation:
	■ Importance of innovation
	■ Models of innovation
	■ Managing innovation

2.2.2	Critically evaluate the appropriateness of developing an international marketing strategy for an organisation investing in international markets:
	▪ Access to low cost materials and labour
	▪ Economies of scale
	▪ Avoiding or bypassing trade barriers
	▪ Access to national/regional incentives eg DFID/Government funding, gateways to strategic markets
2.2.3	Critically evaluate a range of issues that impact on an organisation when entering new countries and markets and consider how they may be managed to achieve the organisation's objectives:
	▪ Extent of global coverage
	▪ Sequence of countries and timing of entry
	▪ Value proposition for global markets
	▪ Standardisation versus customisation
2.2.4	Assess the relevance to an organisation of mergers, acquisitions and strategic alliances in growing, expanding and maximising business potential:
	▪ Motives for strategic alliances
	▪ Types of strategic alliance
	▪ Value chain analysis of the competitive potential in alliances, mergers and acquisitions
2.2.5	Critically evaluate a range of growth strategies for an organisation:
	▪ Incremental growth
	▪ Significant growth
	▪ The concept of big ideas
2.2.6	Critically evaluate the concept of relationship marketing (CRM) as a means of achieving growth and profitability within an organisation:
	▪ Long term orientation versus transactional marketing
	▪ Partnering
	▪ Keeping of promises and developing mutual trust
	▪ Share of customer's wallet versus market share
	▪ Customisation
	▪ Customer loyalty
2.2.7	Critically evaluate the development of an organisation's brand and its contribution towards increasing the organisation's value and brand equity:
	▪ Brand associations
	▪ Brand identity and image
	▪ Brand proposition and promise
	▪ Branding strategies
2.2.8	Critically assess the impact of changing an organisation's strategic position within the market place in order to:
	▪ Reflect the business strategy
	▪ Resonate with customers
	▪ Differentiate from competitors
	▪ Express the values and culture of an organisation in a relevant way
	▪ Express an organisation's corporate social responsibility (CSR), corporate reputation, sustainability and ethics.

Part 3 – Making strategic marketing decisions

3.1 – Making and justifying strategic marketing decisions
(weighting 20% of this part)

3.1.1	Critically assess strategic alternatives against pre-determined criteria for an organisation, including: ■ Scenario planning – stability versus uncertainty ■ Potential for Return on Investment (ROI) ■ Opportunity to achieve competitive advantage ■ Feasibility, viability and resource ■ Capacity and capability to deliver
3.1.2	Assess an organisation's readiness for developing a global strategy including: ■ Strategic importance of the market ■ Position of competitors internationally ■ Cost effectiveness ■ Barriers to trade

3.2 – Financial assessment of marketing opportunities (weighting 30% of this part)

3.2.1	Utilising a range of financial tools, assess the financial benefits and risks for an organisation when selecting from its strategic options: ■ Ratios (INITIAL Financial Descriptors), eg Return on Investment (ROI) ■ Investment Appraisal Techniques, eg Payback, Net Present Value (NPV), Discounted Cash Flows (DCF), Internal Rate of Return (IRR) ■ Cost of capital and Weighted Average Cost of Capital (WACC)
3.2.2	Critically evaluate the source of funds appropriate to the strategic marketing choice and the long-term sustainability and impact of their utilisation: ■ The concept of the cost of capital ■ Capital Asset Pricing Model (CAPM) ■ Weighted Average Cost of Capital (WACC) ■ Optimal capital structure
3.2.3	Assess the impact of the strategic choice upon the shareholder value of organisations in different contexts: ■ The concept of shareholder value-added ■ Cash flow based valuation methods ■ Economic value methods ■ Financial value drivers ■ Timing, sustainability and risk factors in financial valuation
3.2.4	Assess the impact on the economic value of an organisation arising from specific decisions on expenditures/cash flows: ■ The concept of economic value added ■ Cash flow based valuation methods ■ Financial value drivers

The Chartered Institute of Marketing

3.3 – Corporate and reputational risk of marketing decisions – (weighting 30% of this part)

3.3.1	Utilising a range of risk analysis tools, assess the strategic risks facing an organisation in the selection of strategic alternatives leading to strategic choice:
	■ Risk of strategic uncertainty
	■ Risk of diverting from core business, vision and core competencies
	■ Risk of changing technology and capability
	■ Risk of reputation visibility and vulnerability
	■ Financial risk, including shareholder value, investment, liability and loss
3.3.2	Assess the potential for organisational constraints to limit an organisation's success in using any given strategic choice:
	■ Regulation
	■ Structure and competencies
	■ Capital and investment capability
	■ Stakeholder/shareholder engagement and involvement
	■ Competitor activity
3.3.3	Assess the risk to an organisation of hostile or declining markets and recommend mitigation strategies, including:
	■ Milk, harvest, divest, liquidate, consolidate
	■ Review margins and develop stronger cost structures
	■ Reduce potential for proliferation of the product and/or brand
	■ Manage share-shifting
	■ Focus on customer
3.3.4	Recommend a range of mitigation strategies designed to reduce risks, so as to enhance an organisation's selection of a strategic option:
	■ Scenario planning
	■ Forecasting
	■ Changing approach/direction
	■ Avoidance strategies

3.4 – Impact analysis of strategic marketing decisions - (weighting 20% of this part)

3.4.1	Critically analyse the impact of the priority decisions on an organisation:
	■ Strategic vision and direction
	■ The organisation's value proposition
	■ The key success factors
	■ Assets and competencies
	■ Positioning, segmentation and targeting
	■ Distribution
	■ Branding
	■ Investment
	■ Innovation
	■ Manufacturing
	■ Increased opportunities and threats
	Note: in the near future, we can expect a revised syllabus with greater emphasis on digital.

2 The exam paper

2.1 What is the Analysis and Decision case study?

The Analysis and Decision syllabus is examined by a case study, normally comprising many pages of narrative, charts and tables and issued to examinees by post several weeks in advance of the examination. The issue of the case study some weeks in advance allows time for in-depth analysis and discussion. You are required to produce a detailed analysis of the case material in advance of the examination (six sides of A4 maximum, no smaller than font size 11, with tables in font size 8). Marks are awarded for how the candidate **uses** the analysis in the examination, **not** for the analysis itself.

In the exam you will be presented with additional information and the question requirements. The first question will be worth 50 marks, and the other two are worth 25 marks each. All of these questions are compulsory.

The case study is a practical test of the candidates' knowledge of marketing at a strategic level gained across their Postgraduate Diploma studies and their ability to apply it. Normally candidates will also have some practical experience in marketing to bring to bear. At the same time, some background knowledge is necessary. The case study is a culmination of the application of all the marketing knowledge they have gained over several years.

The examiners are looking for candidates to demonstrate analytical ability, interpretive skills, insight, innovation and creativity in answering questions. They are also looking for candidates to take clear and sensible decisions within the context of the case study. A critical awareness of the specific issues involved, relevant theoretical underpinning, attention to detail, coherence and justification of strategies adopted will also be assessed.

To perform well on the paper, candidates will have to exhibit the following:

- The ability to concentrate on the strategic aspects of marketing underpinned by the necessary detail
- The ability to identify 'gaps' in the case study and to outline the assumptions made
- The ability to critically apply relevant models for case analysis
- The ability to draw and synthesise from any of the diploma subject areas as relevant
- Concentration on the question set, rather than any pre-prepared answer
- The ability to answer in the required format, with comprehensive sentences rather than providing simplistic lists
- The judicious use of diagrams for illustrative purposes
- The ability to draw disparate links together and give coherent answers
- Innovation and creativity in answering questions
- Demonstration of practical applications of marketing knowledge
- Sensible use of time and an ability to plan the answer within the set time
- A good understanding of the case study set
- The ability to suggest appropriate control mechanisms and contingency plans

2.2 Discussing the case study

Students are strongly advised to conduct in-depth discussion with colleagues on the case study analysis and its issues. This can be accomplished by forming syndicate groups of four to six people and the holding of frequent sessions where all candidates gather together. In this way a much more balanced, integrated and secure approach can be developed.

You are allowed to take pre-prepared pages of analysis. It is useful to work with others on the analysis if possible, but the decisions made need to be your own. You must believe in your recommendations and be able to justify them in order to come across credibly in the exam.

2.3 Problems to avoid

The case is a challenging assessment method. Knowledge and understanding are tested but so are your practical skills of analysis and decision-making. Your recommendations must be presented persuasively to influence your audiences – the examiner, and the organisation you are advising.

Like any exam, practise is the key to success. Here are some likely problems that you need to be able to avoid.

Problems in balancing the allocation of time

A balance needs to be struck between preliminary analysis, answer planning, and actually writing the required answers. It is a good idea to try to answer past cases under simulated examination conditions, and learn to pace yourself over the time available. You should take no more than 30 minutes to read the unseen part of the exam and plan the answer.

Excess attention on pre-seen material and insufficient attention to unseen data

You need to fully absorb the changes outlined in the unseen material, and avoid the temptation to base your answer solely on the pre-seen material. For example, SWOTs prepared from the pre-seen case need to take into account any significant changes outlined in the unseen material. Rote-learned lists of potential issues are not enough – you need to hone your skills in the rapid analysis and absorption of new data, and the clear identification of new developments.

Failing to read, interpret and hence answer the exact requirement

Do not place too much reliance on forecasting the likely question, and effectively answering that question rather than dealing with the specific requirement. Read the requirement carefully!

Candidates should realise that there will always be a range of possible unseen issues and questions to follow any given pre-seen. However, there is always the temptation for individual candidates or lecturers to concentrate on one 'most likely' question. Candidates should review pre-seen material with great caution. The unseen part need not develop all of the issues that might have been identified in the pre-seen.

The wording of the requirement provides clear guidance to the expected form of the answer.

Standard of presentation

Your written English needs to be fluent, concise and easy to understand. Report layouts need to be clear.

Providing recommendations

Your recommendations need to be supported by appropriate reasons. The weakest part of many answers is often in the recommendations. Problems appear in two forms:

(a) Candidates not providing firm recommendations. You will have to accept that information is imperfect, but you cannot ignore the requirement to offer recommendations.

(b) Candidates not providing reasons for recommendations. Any requirement to give recommendations implies that reasons should be given. A sensible approach might be to summarise those aspects of the detailed analysis that support a recommendation into a list of bullet points. You cannot expect the reader of your report to reach the same conclusions as you do without some guidance through your deliberations. Marks will be allowed where it is clear from the analysis why certain courses of action are being recommended.

Financial analysis

It is reasonably feasible to forecast a range of techniques that may be useful in the examination from the pre-seen information, and these techniques should be revised to ensure competent application to the pre-seen numbers and any new numbers provided on the day of the examination. The pre-seen numbers should be analysed prior to the examination.

While case studies may lead at times to a need for a project appraisal, it would be unwise to assume that this is an inevitable requirement. Other calculations may be needed, and the appropriate test of skills at this level is not of skills in processing numbers in set ways, but in understanding which calculations may be appropriate.

2.4 Exam technique

Exam technique is rather different for a case exam, but nonetheless requires practise and the development of a wide range of skills already alluded to, from analysis to persuasive communication, skills which you would expect to find in a competent, practising marketing manager.

Exam technique for the case study starts when the exam case is issued. Finding enough time for preparation and using that time effectively is all part of case technique. The seeds of success or failure are sown during this important preparation time.

By now, a number of CIM examinations will be successfully under your belt, and the general tips on exam technique all remain equally valid. However, even strong minds can go blank in the pressures of an exam room so the following notes will remind you of best exam practice to ensure you do not throw away a case study through poor presentation or exam technique.

Get organised

Make sure you have space and materials such as files and dividers so you can organise your notes and analysis as soon as the case comes.

You may find the idea of having blank templates of key models helpful (you may photocopy those provided in the study text). You can simply add the case detail to these as you come across them.

Developing an exam timetable

You should have already allocated time for the case study preparation following advice given by the CIM. Use the timetable that follows to help you monitor your case preparation.

Case Step 1:	Read and overview case
Case Step 2:	Complete internal review analysis
Case Step 3:	Complete external review analysis
Case Step 4:	Prioritise and identify critical success factors and prepare analysis summary
Case Step 5:	Establishing the strategic direction
Case Step 6:	Consider marketing management and business implications
Case Step 7:	Develop marketing strategies and marketing mix plans
Case Step 8:	Develop contemporary issues and management plans
Case Step 9:	Develop controls
Case Step 10:	Preparing for the exam

Adequate analysis will ensure you have a sound grasp of the case issues and have the facts and figures needed to support your recommendations and convince the examiner of their commercial credibility.

Moving on from analysis to decision-making is another exam challenge for case students. Analysis can be comforting; you are busy doing something and there is almost always something else that could be done. Before the examination day, however, you really need to be at the point where you have a broad picture of the strategic options open to the business, and which options you would support in what circumstances. The emphasis at this level of your studies is on helping the organisation to determine:

- Which products and markets to serve
- The competitive strategy likely to be most effective in winning business from these markets
- Which segments of the selected markets to target
- How best to deploy the marketing mix to gain a competitive advantage within these segments
- The implications for the organisation and management
- The challenges of implementation
- Contemporary issues

2.5 Comments from the Senior Examiner (on the June 2012 exam, The News International Case)

'Throughout the assessment, candidates were expected to show a good understanding and knowledge of relevant concepts from a range of syllabus areas (eg, analysis of strategic position, core competencies and competitive positioning, evaluation of capabilities and constraints in the context of strategic intent, assessment of strategic options, recommendations and justification of option, evaluating the significance of corporate governance and leadership and the way in which organisational culture could contribute to success and minimise risks). However, simple knowledge of basic concepts was not enough as candidates were expected to evaluate and apply to the given context, providing sufficient details. Hence, more marks were available for application and evaluation than for simple understanding of basic theory and concepts'.

In his report, the Senior Examiner refers to the fact that candidates' strengths derived mostly from a realistic appraisal of the situation and the possible options facing a mature company like News International, in a declining market: 'the stronger scripts showed an ability to use academic theory and models to demonstrate and justify the rationale behind the thinking, demonstrating a mature understanding of the wider issues'.

According to the Senior Examiner, the six-page audit needed to demonstrate individual effort, independent thinking and thoughtful insights, including reference to

- A range of techniques and /or models to assess the macro as well as the micro-environment and a resource-based view of News International, including an analysis of their approach to customer value and the way the company is developing further resources and capabilities.

- An understanding of strategic uncertainty and risks

- The way that strategic options have been formulated, with especial mention of brand leverage through the use of models such as Porter's Five Forces Framework

2.6 Reasons for poor results

The overall pass rate for the June 2012 exam was only 42%. For the more than half of the candidates who did not pass, the Senior Examiner offers the following advice.

'There were two key issues. Firstly, the ability to provide sufficient details, insights and rigour expected at the postgraduate level appeared to be the key differentiating factor between those who did and those who did not perform well. Whilst there is no set standard, it is challenging for examiners to award 25 marks to a piece of work that covers less than two sides. Secondly, those who covered the syllabus in its entirety were able to perform well. For instance, only the good candidates were able to cover all three tasks in sufficient depth'.

Task Three, says the Senior Examiner, was the weakest – perhaps because of the lack of time- with many struggling to identify the key focus of the tasks. The lack of depth of analysis, the paucity of evaluation and application fell short of what is expected at the postgraduate level.

Task One (a) was the best answered overall (once more, this could indicate that time management was a problem). 'Good candidates showed reasonable understanding of core competencies and competitive positioning...'

Note: the full report is available on the CIM website.

THE REAL WORLD

Dyson concentrates on distinctive capabilities and core competence

In their paper *The Core Competence of the Organization* (1990), Hamel & Prahalad put forward the notion that companies should spend time assessing and developing their distinctive capabilities and essential competence to achieve differentiation.

According to the authors, there is a test of three factors that can be applied to determine core competencies.

Firstly, the feature should give access to a wide variety of markets and not target a limited niche with few buyers.

Secondly, the competence, or skill, should be of significant benefit to Customers.

Finally, it should be preferably quite unique and difficult, impractical or even impossible, for others to imitate.

James Dyson is the inventive genius behind the British based company Dyson, which was set up in 1993, revolutionising the vacuum cleaner market. Dyson cleaners, although generally more expensive than competing models, are extremely efficient, lightweight and colourful, dispensing with the need for a bag to collect dust. Inventiveness, 21st century design and efficiency in operation (including enhanced manoeuvrability) are all distinctive capabilities that make Dyson stand out from the crowd.

From 2009, Dyson began implementing other air-powered technologies, for example the AirBlade hand drier, the bladeless fan and Dyson Hot, the bladeless fan heater.

Could any of this technology be easily copied? The Air Multiplier, for example, has a deceptively simple structure but results from a complicated design procedure. One Dyson design engineer was quoted by Time Magazine as saying: 'We have many patents on this [fan], on the impeller, aerofoil and product development'. In October, 2012, Dyson is pursuing Bosch in the courts for a case of alleged industrial spying. http://www.time.com/time/health/article/0,8599,1931455,00.html#ixzz22eBdjECh

Starting from a workshop behind his house Sir James Dyson, the inventor of cyclone technology as applied to vacuum cleaners, employed over 3000 people and operated in 50 countries in 2012.

---

3 Sample examination case study: Ryanair

In preparation for the examination, you will need to analyse the organisation, on the basis of the case material provided. Your written analysis **should not exceed six A4 pages**.

Candidates are encouraged to use a range of analytical tools and models in order to undertake a thorough investigation of the key aspects of the case.

Clearly, the analysis required will vary depending on the specific case content but, as a guide, consider undertaking the following activities for the sample case study, Ryanair.

- SWOT analysis – internal and external
- Value chain analysis
- Analysis of the external environment using PEST analysis
- Analysis of the competitive environment using Porter's Five Forces model
- Strategic review using Ansoff's matrix and/or Porter's generic strategies
- Detailed review/analysis of the marketing mix elements
- Analysing any financial information

 The Chartered Institute of Marketing

A previous case study used by CIM covered the airline industry, specifically Ryanair. In the sample case study, you are undertaking the role of a Marketing Consultant with a specialist interest in the airline sector.

Case Study, *Ryanair*

Currently (2012), with a fleet of nearly 300 aircraft and revenues of €4.3bn, Ryanair, based in Ireland, was the first 'Budget Airline' to operate in Europe. With its origins in 1985 as a regional airline, Ryanair started operations on the Dublin-London route, initially with fares as much as 50% cheaper than major players British Airways and Aer Lingus. In its first full year of operation, Ryanair carried 82,000 passengers.

From 1987, more routes were added between the UK and Ireland. 1988 saw the opening of the first two continental routes to Munich and Brussels. This initial success was short-lived as both its Business Class Service and its Frequent Flyer Club were failures and were phased out before 1990.

Taking as a model the hugely successful American airline Southwest – and after accruing losses of £20 million because of over-expansion and the 'fare wars' with the other airlines – Ryanair was re-launched under new management as Europe's first low fares airline.

This typical Case Study, from 2009, is no longer available on CIM's website, although your Tutor may have a copy. The contents of the Ryanair case study are as follows:

- Industry sector background
- History of deregulation
- The low cost business model
- Introduction of extra costs
- Description of LCCs (budget airlines, referred to as Low-Cost Carriers) and airports
- Effect of the credit crunch
- Analysis of the major players – EasyJet, Air Berlin, Ryanair
- Ryanair profits
- The future
- Extracts from Ryanair's annual report

Do not be surprised if the material seems muddled at first. As you work with it and sort it into relevant groups it will start to make more sense. Do avoid rushing into *ad hoc* analysis: it pays to work through the case thoroughly and logically, so that you can be sure that you have stripped out all the relevant data. We will use the bullet points above as our guide for your programme of analysis of the Ryanair case study.

3.1 SWOT analysis – internal factors

For the results of the audit to be of any value, SWOT must be prioritised in order to ensure that the organisation is focused on those issues that matter most; for example, the weaknesses and threats that will impact upon organisational success.

A long list of SWOT might provide an improved understanding of the current situation, but it can be a daunting step to move from this list to decisions. There are also always constraints on resources, money, time, processes and people, and so priorities must be established to determine what is important and must be invested in, and what can wait.

Strengths – route network; 'lowest fares' reputation; world's largest international airline; huge cash balance; large fleet of aircraft, including fuel-efficient models; best on-time performance; willingness to employ aggressive tactics such as free seat giveaways; low cost base; low net debt; aggressive management ready to exploit downturns, lower costs and increase efficiency.

Weaknesses – these are less easy to pinpoint – maybe the perceived level of customer service (compared to EasyJet?)

BPP
LEARNING MEDIA

3.2 Value chain analysis

The traditional airlines have, in the main, a vertically integrated service with many activities such as baggage handling, ticketing and maintenance delivered by their own subsidiaries. Additionally, they have continued to offer a variety of classes ranging from luxury to economy, thus catering for all segments of the travelling market.

By contrast, the budget airlines have concentrated on the short-haul market and have heavily promoted low-cost flights to secondary airports with no service other than the flight. These low costs have been partially supported by subsidies provided by the secondary airports. An additional advantage of these airports is the rapid turnaround of aircraft on the ground, since they are handling fewer flights. Aircrew, at minimum permitted staffing levels, are responsible for aircraft cleaning. The budget price includes only the flight; LCCs seek to maximise revenue from their passengers by offering no (or very few) in-flight services, and passengers book their tickets directly via the Internet (the cheapest channel, which also offers the opportunity to cross-sell services such as hotel bookings and insurance). The budget airlines spend heavily on advertising in all popular media.

Low cost airlines are giving the customers what they want (low cost air travel, opening up air travel to people who may not have thought that they could afford to fly overseas) and they are able to do this by exploiting their assets through their particular business model:

- Modern fleets
- Single class cabins
- Point-to-point routes (reduced complexity)
- Few frills, with 'extras' charged for
- Direct sales (online, with no use of travel agents)
- Good fleet utilisation
- Use of secondary airports
- Simple ground facilities
- Short haul only
- Performance-based compensation for employees

Recently some of the LCCs have started charging for services such as checking-in of baggage (other than hand luggage) and priority boarding. There is strict cost control in all areas to counteract increasing fuel prices – fuel efficient aircraft, hedging strategies, pay freezes, redundancies, renegotiated supply contracts, increased discretionary charges.

3.3 Analysis of the external environment – opportunities, threats and PEST analysis

What are the priority issues in Ryanair's external environment? We can consider the three Cs of the dynamic new business environment – customers (who are more demanding), competition (nature and intensity; 60 LCCs operating in Europe) and industry change (a constant).

Ryanair operates in an industry where margins are negligible and risks very high. Long-term investment is necessary but does improve this year's quarterly results. Investment in new technology takes place in profitable times, and consolidation in the form of alliances, takeovers and mergers is a common trend. It is a risky sector. Immediately, this gives a crucial insight into the nature of the industry and a host of strategic issues that a company such as Ryanair is likely to deal with.

Opportunities: One way of increasing revenue that has been identified is to charge passengers for certain services (such as airport check-in and baggage other than hand luggage, and priority boarding). LCCs are becoming more like online travel agents, with offerings such as car hire and hotel bookings. The 'Open Skies' agreement of March 2008 has opened up the airline market like never before – the setting up of a transatlantic route is under consideration, using aircraft from the hoped-for acquisition of Aer Lingus. Elsewhere, new geographical markets such as southern and eastern Europe offer growth opportunities and in-flight mobile

telephony is being considered. To quote the annual report 'this is a cyclical industry, and a downturn in the industry provides enormous opportunity for airlines such as Ryanair.'

Threats: while capacity is growing, with LCCs being a major driver of growth in the European travel market, the low cost part of the market may be reaching maturity and growth is likely to slow in Ireland and the UK. This represents a threat to Ryanair, as does the improvement in land-based travel with increased investment in railway infrastructure, for example. Pressure from environmentalists to cut carbon emissions is another area of increasing costs for European airlines – air carriers are included in the EU's emissions trading scheme. In the UK, airport regulation is under the control of the BAA, which operates as a monopoly and has imposed large increases in airport charges. Ryanair's promise never to impose fuel surcharges could be interpreted as a threat as it limits the ability to cover costs fully, but if it can be sustained it becomes an opportunity to lure cost-conscious customers away from competitors.

PEST analysis:

Political:	Deregulation of the market helping to open it up (fewer restrictions imposed upon fares and routes by national authorities); takeover of Aer Lingus blocked by the European Commission; BAA monopoly in the UK and at Dublin airport.
Economic:	Adverse currency movements (weaker pound sterling) may discourage travel from the UK; effect of the credit crunch; record fuel costs are hitting the industry hard, and increased airport charges (both out of the company's control).
Social:	Low cost air travel is now competing with other everyday purchases, on a par with buying clothes. Europe has opened up for people who previously did not think that they could afford to travel by air. There is some evidence that the credit crunch is not affecting demand for cheap air travel.
Technological:	Huge reliance on online bookings – encouraged via charging passengers who do not use it!

3.4 Analysis of the competitive environment using Porter's Five Forces model

A competitor analysis is essential to any future strategy. Sort out who is active in the LCC market and what strategies they are adopting. The sample case study gives us information about EasyJet and Air Berlin, and it is easy to note some differences straight away.

EasyJet takes far more pride in its treatment of its customers: 'low cost with care and convenience… we continue to eliminate the unnecessary costs and frills… but provide a friendly on-board service'. In many respects, however, its business model is identical to that of Ryanair. Ryanair makes no claims about its customer service – it concentrates almost 100% on being the cheapest (whatever that entails for the customer's experience of the airline).

Air Berlin, based in Germany, is unusual amongst the LCCs in that it still uses third party intermediaries (travel agents). Like Ryanair, it is aiming for the long-haul market and global business travel. Again, like Ryanair, it has followed a policy of growth through acquisition.

Porter's five forces model can be used to analyse the competitiveness, level of profitability and attractiveness of an industry and the firm's competitive position within the industry.

Bargaining power of customers – increasingly uncertain in uncertain economic times.

Bargaining power of suppliers – Ryanair has renegotiated certain supply contracts and is taking on the airport operators, accusing them of overcharging and choking the industry.

The threat of entrants – in the air travel business, the barriers to entry have been relatively high because of high capital costs of aircraft; regulation of routes and landing slots has restricted access; government affection for, and ownership of, national flag carriers; and the restrictions on airport services.

Competitive rivalry – there are around 60 LCCs operating in Europe, but Ryanair is only really 'threatened' in terms of size by EasyJet and Air Berlin.

Substitutes – SouthWest Airlines (Ryanair's model) regards the motor car as its key substitute. Railways in Europe also offer competition on short and medium haul routes.

Every market will differ in its characteristics. However, the following general analytical framework can be applied to most markets or segments. You should identify the following for Ryanair:

- The size of the market
- Whether the market is growing, stable or declining
- How the market is segmented?
- To what extent each segment is growing, stable or declining
- The key players in the market/segments (eg manufacturers, travel agents etc).
- The key success factors in this market or segment
- The buying behaviour characteristics of this market/segment
- The major market/segment competitors, their distinctive competences
- Future environmental factors affecting this market/segment
- How easy or difficult is the market and/or segment to enter or exit

3.5 Strategic review using Ansoff's matrix and/or Porter's generic strategies

Over the past few years, the major airlines have suffered a decline in profitability and some have even filed for bankruptcy. At the same time, budget airlines (LCCs) such as Ryanair have shown considerable success offering a 'no frills service' to an increasing number of passengers at heavily discounted fares. Using the analysis provided by Porter's generic competitive strategies, they are 'low cost' and Ryanair has even reiterated its promise not to impose fuel surcharges even with the current unprecedented fuel prices.

Possible growth strategies for Ryanair include (referring to Ansoff's matrix):

Figure 2.1   Ansoff's matrix

Market penetration strategy	Product development strategy
1 More purchasing and usage from existing customers	1 Product modification via new features
2 Gain customers from competitors	2 Different quality levels
3 Convert non-users into users	3 'New' product/route
Market development strategy	**Diversification strategy**
1 New market segments	1 Organic growth
2 New distribution channels	2 Joint ventures
3 New geographic areas eg New York	3 Mergers
	4 Acquisition/take-over

Critical success factors (CSF) are those factors that will affect the organisation's ability to pursue the opportunities it has identified and intends to implement. Critical success factors are any factors essential to the success of organisation and strategy.

- Profitability and cash flow
- Market development and market position
- Productivity

The Chartered Institute of Marketing

- Identifying/developing competitive advantage and new product development
- Marketing orientation, employee attitudes and public responsibility
- Marketing management skills and personnel leadership
- Competitive positioning and product leadership – first air line to introduce the 'low fares' model

Ryanair's main strategy is to slash fares in order to stimulate demand and expand the customer base, and to promote its new routes. It is more aggressive than others – some airlines have decided to cut back on capacity and reduce their growth strategies, but Ryanair 'will... continue to grow, by lowering fares, taking market share from competitors, and expanding in markets where competitors either withdraw capacity or go bust.'

Its customer service metrics are punctuality, lost bags and cancellations (all quantifiable and objective). There is no mention of customer satisfaction surveys or other more subjective measures.

3.6 Detailed review/analysis of the marketing mix elements

Ryanair needs to assess how customers are changing: what are the emerging needs or concerns?

Discounts such as free seat giveaways, or increased advertising, might increase sales revenue and total profit but will depress gross profit margins. Decisions to change any element of the marketing mix will have financial consequences: marketers need to be aware of these and budget for them.

Marketing implications are inevitably interlinked with business implications and are those strategic issues associated with marketing activities which include:

(a) Customer focus (implicit in a marketing orientation and dependent on good marketing intelligence, marketing information systems and the ability to segment markets)

(b) Product/services offered and the quality, benefits and value they represent to the customer (including e.g. accessibility – place, value for money – price)

(c) Customer service (implicit in the people, processes and physical evidence policies)

(d) Communications, positioning and the brand. Positioning is the act of designing the company's offer and image so that it achieves a distinct and valued place in the target customer's mind. Ryanair is emphatically 'low cost' and it is very clearly positioned in the budget air travel market. It is probably no exaggeration to say that nothing says low cost air travel quite like the name 'Ryanair'.

3.7 Analysing financial information

Remember the marketer's effect on gross profit! Marketing decisions directly influence the gross profit margins of the business. Appreciating the implications of your decisions is critical to your ability to share responsibility for the financial health of the business. There has been criticism of marketers' lack of financial skills and the Senior Examiners have made it clear that this area will be tested.

We appreciate most marketers hate the thought of numbers, but it is essential. One of the questions on the sample case study paper refers to the 'financial challenges' facing Ryanair and other operators in the low-cost carrier market. One of the most obvious challenges is the surging cost of fuel, which is the largest line item in the company's profit and loss account – 40% of operating costs.

Using the financial information in the Ryanair case study, the following ratios can be employed for the year to March 2008 (note that we do not have any balance sheet information and that financial information in this sample case study is actually fairly limited):

Profitability ratios

- Profit after tax – up 20%
- Sales revenue – up 21%
- Revenue per passenger – 2007 = 52.6 Euro; 2008 = 53.3 Euro

3.8 Conclusion

There are no single correct answers to a case study, so the examiner will not have fixed ideas about the right strategy. What he or she will be looking for is evidence that you have worked through a logical process resulting in:

- Clear decision making
- Justified decisions
- Convincing arguments in favour of those decisions

If you are not confident about the recommendations you are making, it is unlikely you would convince the case organisation or the examiner. The successful selling of strategy in business is being directly tested in how you present your proposals.

Refer to our suggested answers to the sample case study questions in the next section.

4 Suggested answer to sample examination case study: Ryanair

▶ **Assessment tip**

Our suggested answer takes the form of a three-part report, each part addressing, in turn, the three tasks on the examination paper.

REPORT

To: Ryanair Board

From: Marketing Consultant

Date: December 20XX

I have been asked to prepare a report on the strategic options available to Ryanair over the short term ie the next three to five years. The report is presented in three parts:

- Part One – Strategic priorities in the next three years
- Part Two – Growth options for the next three to five years
- Part Three – Should Ryanair reposition itself?

4.1 Part One – Strategic priorities

The macroeconomic environment for the airline industry is worsening. European LCCs are facing the challenge of higher fuel prices, rising fees at airports, falling consumer demand and the current economic downturn, with uncertain customer demand for airline seats. Ryanair has, to date, been very successful in building its reputation upon slashing fares in order to stimulate traffic to expand the customer base, steal market share and promote new routes.

Strategic priorities for Ryanair must now be centred around survival and growth in a risky sector. As mentioned by the company in its press release, the outlook for the next few years is entirely dependent upon fares and fuel prices. What are Ryanair's options in these areas? Future strategy for Ryanair will be built upon its core strengths and competences – its low cost base, it huge cash reserves of over 2 billion euro, and its low fares. Some form of scenario planning, factoring in the uncertainties mentioned in the first paragraph, would be an extremely useful exercise.

The company, through its aggressive growth to date, has developed a habit of being able to turn situations to its advantage, influencing the future by controlling its impact – if oil prices remain high, Ryanair expects to be able to take advantage of higher-charging competitors withdrawing capacity or going bust by taking over their

The Chartered
Institute of Marketing

routes. If oil prices go down, then Ryanair's earnings will rebound. Ryanair seems sure that weaker LCCs will cut back capacity or trim their growth strategies. Some will go into administration, or be acquired by major players, whilst the growth rate of the low fare airline sector will slow because the market is nearing saturation in some areas.

Ryanair needs to maintain its strong name in a sector with lots of competition. There are over 60 LCCs in Europe, although only EasyJet and Air Berlin are of comparable size. Their competitive positioning must be kept under review so that they do not overtake Ryanair's strong 'low fares' position.

The market is reaching maturity in the UK and Ireland, so Ryanair needs to be part of new opportunities to counteract any threat from other modes of travel, such as railways. It needs to identify new routes, such as those abandoned by other airlines as being uneconomic for them to operate and continue to grow capacity via network development and aircraft acquisition. New geographical markets, such as Southern and Eastern Europe, are projected to treble their spending in this sector over the next ten years. Ryanair has a history of dealings with Tarom, the Romanian airline.

Part of any innovation must be the identification of new revenue streams and new opportunities for cost-cutting and flexibility. Perhaps the reintroduction of business class and frequent flyer clubs, having abandoned them in the past before Ryanair was the size that it is now, would help to drive revenue. This would entail a move away from the current business model, where having a single class cabin means reduced cabin crew costs and more seats per plane. Given the current economic uncertainty, developing a competence in business class traffic may not be a strength, but a weakness. Business traffic has dried up with companies slashing their travel budgets. With so many empty seats, traditional airlines have been falling over themselves to offer discounts of as much as 70% in business class. Looking ahead, it is unlikely to get much brighter, certainly in the short term.

Other initiatives being considered, that could be developed over the short term, are charges for mobile telephony, bingo, gaming and entertainment, and charges for the use of credit cards. No information has been provided on the costs and revenues associated with these initiatives. Management would need to be convinced that such strategies would not be loss making.

Ryanair should continue to promote and encourage the online channel for more cross selling opportunities; it is cheaper than the model employed by Air Berlin, as evidenced by the latter's falling profitability in recent years. According to Ryanair, 'the more passengers we convert to web check-in and carry-on luggage only, the more we can reduce our airport and handling costs and pass on these savings in the form of lower air fares'.

This means, however, embracing the online environment and all its implications, including the operation of third party websites that can sell Ryanair tickets. This will complement developments in the online travel sector, where Ryanair and EasyJet have both signed agreements with major operators.

Ryanair must take advantage of smaller airports as they are built – identify where these are going to be developed over the next few years. LCCs are increasingly in the position that they can 'call the shots' and influence airport facilities' design.

Does Ryanair have a 'marketing orientation'? Should there be a greater focus upon customers and the 'customer experience'? This is not something that Ryanair is necessarily associated with. Customer service metrics that are used are valuable but they are purely quantifiable ones (level of 'on time' performance, number of cancellations and levels of lost baggage) that do not take account of more quantitative measures such as 'customer satisfaction'. Is Ryanair absolutely sure that customers are only interested in low fares 'at any price'? EasyJet probably has a better reputation in this area, although in most other areas the business models of Ryanair and EasyJet are identical – internet sales, investment in new aircraft and high asset utilisation, low cost ticketless travel, no frills and efficient use of airports.

If we consider EasyJet's statement that it aims to improve its operating margins and return on equity 'by a combination of network development and optimisation, ancillary revenue growth and concentrated cost control', this sounds very similar to the approach favoured by Ryanair.

Ryanair's growth has been largely organic, with the addition of new routes and the purchase or leasing of new aircraft, growing to become the largest international airline in the world some 22 years after it first began operating as a regional Irish airline. One acquisition (Buzz, from KLM) was made in 2003. The pace of aircraft acquisition has been dramatic, with 133 aircraft now flying 649 routes.

An effective management is a key organisation resource in planning activities, controlling the organisation and motivating staff. Ryanair's management is not afraid to take tough decisions – closing loss making activities and undergoing a major restructuring along the lines of the Southwest Airlines business model. Southwest Airlines is one of the most profitable in the US, partly because it defined its competition carefully. Most airlines in the US have a 'hub' airport and 'spokes' from it. They compete with each other heavily on matters such as air miles and price. Southwest prefers to fly 'point to point' over short distances. It has defined its competitor as the motor car – a substitute product – and has designed its marketing mix to minimise the time the customer takes travelling. This has meant flying from smaller, less congested airports and speeded-up check-in times – a revolutionary model when it was first conceived.

Ryanair is characterised by flexibility – when the Gulf War affected air travel in 1991, Ryanair closed some routes, disposed of some aircraft and moved to London Stansted because of better rail links with the capital.

With the considerable economic uncertainty, the company needs to maintain this flexibility and ability to make tough decisions – salary freezes, redundancies, contract renegotiations, downsizing and grounding of aircraft are all mentioned. The cost structure is volatile, with fuel now accounting for 40% of costs. There are many routes to cost advantage (Aaker, 2007). They include, for Ryanair:

- Economies of scale through its large fleet and network

- The experience curve – over 20 years in business

- Product design innovations – the original and uncompromising 'low cost' airline, now with cheaper and fuel efficient aircraft

- The use of 'no-frills' offerings

Pressure to cut carbon emissions is another area where costs will increase, due to the inclusion of airlines in the European Union's Emissions Trading Scheme. This issue is addressed more fully in Part Three of this report.

Guaranteeing no fuel surcharges is admirable, and the level of cash held by the company means that they can afford it at the moment, but can this be sustained if the fuel price continues to climb?

Consolidation among airlines in Europe continues, but the acquisition of Aer Lingus is unlikely to be achieved in the short term, although Ryanair should continue to lobby for the reversal of the European Commission's decision. This acquisition seems to represent the next logical step in the development of Ryanair and its evolution into a strong Irish airline group, and will enable it to operate the new long haul route to New York using aircraft that Aer Lingus has on order. Entry into the long haul market is an attractive option, with the Open Skies agreement enabling unfettered access to North American routes.

The last words come from the Ryanair press release:

'The airlines who will survive this period of higher oil prices and industry downturn are those with new cheaper fuel efficient aircraft, lower costs, substantial cash balances, low net debt and management who are ready to exploit downturns to drive costs lower and increase efficiency. No airline is better placed in Europe than Ryanair to trade through this downturn. We will therefore continue to grow, by lowering fares, taking market share from competitors, and expanding in markets where competitors either withdraw capacity or go bust. We believe that our earnings will rebound strongly when oil prices settle down as we believe they will, and in the interim we will take the tough decisions necessary to lower our costs in this difficult period.'

The Chartered Institute of Marketing

4.2 Part Two – Growth options

▶ **Assessment tip**

Refer back to your case study analysis where you should have produced an Ansoff matrix of growth options (see 3.5). You need to make reasoned proposals that allow Ryanair to extend its operations beyond its current services. It is extremely important to be realistic in making your suggestions.

Ansoff's product market matrix is a familiar framework to adopt in the generation of growth options, reiterating:

Market penetration strategy

1   More purchasing and usage from existing customers
2   Gain customers from competitors

Market development strategy

1   New market segments
2   New distribution channels – online development
3   New geographic areas eg New York route, Eastern Europe

Product development strategy

1   Product modification via new routes
2   Different quality levels – business class?

Diversification strategy

1   Organic growth to date
2   Joint ventures
3   Mergers
4   Acquisition/take-over of Aer Lingus

Strategy is a pattern of senior management decisions, arising out of the general management process whereby senior managers direct and control the business.

This general management process tends to generate consistent decisions, within the constraints that are operating and according to the resources that are available.

The growth options available to Ryanair are constrained by financial challenges and risks identified in Part One of the report.

- High fuel costs
- Higher airport costs
- Uncertain customer demand
- Economic downturn
- Level of competitor fares
- Huge levels of investment required
- Blockage of proposed acquisitions (eg that of Aer Lingus, by the European Commission)

The choice of strategy for Ryanair should follow a strategic logic:

- It must be consistently related to the objectives of Ryanair

- It must match the organisation's capability (including its structure, control systems and culture) to its environment

Looking at some of the options identified above:

(a)   Different quality levels, such as the introduction of business class, as a form of product development, is not achievable without redesigning the 'low cost carrier' model, and varying the company's 'lowest fare' position. This could confuse the position of Ryanair in the mind of the customer.

(b)   The design of new distribution channels as a form of market development – Ryanair already relies heavily on application of the Internet, and this is the lowest cost channel. Developing online agreements with travel operators could help to drive growth.

(c)   Organic growth – this has been the pattern to date, but is likely to slow down considerably with uncertain market conditions over the next three to five years.

(d)   By contrast, strategic alliances speed market penetration, normally by providing extra distribution effort. Many firms are expanding through alliances. For example, some of the traditional airlines have code sharing arrangements, which give them access to a larger base of assets.

Such assets include:

- Market access
- Management skills
- Shared technology
- Exclusivity (eg shutting out competitors)

Joint ventures, mergers and acquisitions by Ryanair are likely to be blocked under the current regulatory regime. Over the next three to five years, elements of a market penetration strategy and market development strategy are more likely to be successful.

Market penetration strategy

Gaining customers from competitors is something that Ryanair has successfully managed throughout its history as its reputation as an aggressively low-cost operator has been consolidated with the growth of its network. The failure of other operators is likely to be a recurring feature of the industry in the near future, with continued uncertainty over fuel costs and uncertain customer demand. Those operators who, unlike Ryanair, cannot afford not to impose fuel surcharges are bound to lose customers to those who can guarantee low fares.

Market development strategy

New routes to North America and southern and eastern Europe will enable Ryanair to attract new customers, given that the markets in Ireland and the UK from existing customers are reaching saturation point. The acquisition of new aircraft should continue as new routes are developed – this has been the company's preferred growth method to date, and its cash balance certainly allows for some investment. New routes could also be regarded as a form of product development.

4.3 Part Three – Repositioning

The following quotes and points are taken from http://news.bbc.co.uk/2/hi/uk_news/politics/6236089.stm

- 'Ryanair has opposed efforts by the EU to control aviation carbon emissions by including them in a trading scheme, saying it would discriminate against low-cost airlines.'

- 'The EU's scheme will see airlines pay for exceeding their current level of emissions.'

- 'Flights within Europe will come under the jurisdiction of the Emissions Trading Scheme by 2011.'

- 'The scheme would be expanded from 2012 to include all international flights that arrive at or depart from an EU airport.'

- 'Airlines would be issued with pollution permits – those that cut emissions would be able to sell their surplus while an airline that increased its emissions would have to buy more permits.'

- 'Toby Nicol, spokesman for Budget airline Easyjet, said the company "stands full-square with the government" on the proposal to include EU internal flights and international flights in the carbon trading scheme.'

> **TASK**
>
> Develop a reasoned argument for and against the proposal that Ryanair should reposition itself, and come down either in favour of repositioning or against it.

> ▶ **Assessment tip**
>
> This task touches on issues of corporate social responsibility, not something that Ryanair is automatically associated with. The question is asked in the context of Ryanair's lack of enthusiasm for the emissions trading scheme.

'Strategic position, the face of the business strategy, specifies how the business aspires to be perceived ... relative to its competitors and market.' (Aaker & McLoughlin, 2007)

A strategic position should be:

(a) Strategic – reflecting the business strategy, and reflecting a long term effort to gain competitive advantage.

(b) Defined relative to competitors and the market – via a point of differentiation where the organisation can position itself.

(c) Resonant with customers – appealing to customers and their perceptions of value.

When Ryanair was accused of being 'the unacceptable face of capitalism', it was by a UK government official commenting on the company's opposition to the inclusion of airlines in the EU's emissions trading scheme.

Ryanair has positioned itself extremely clearly and successfully in the 'low cost carrier' market. Customers know exactly what they are going to get for the price that they pay – that is the simple proposition of the company, and it works. Part of the low cost strategy has been the investment by Ryanair in cheaper and more fuel-efficient aircraft.

This, however, has failed to placate environmental activists and others concerned about the impact of the airline industry on the environment. The EU Emissions Trading Scheme (ETS) attempts to control emissions by making companies that exceed their limits pay for their excess pollution, while those that do not can sell their unused pollution quota. Ryanair claims that such an arrangement will discriminate against low cost airlines, although it seems that EasyJet is quite happy to play along.

So we can see that at times the performance (or at least the perception) of a brand might falter, and managers can attempt to rectify the situation if they see the need. Strategic managers must be prepared to deal with perceived under performance in certain areas, even if they are not areas that primarily concern the company. The perception of stakeholders (government officials, green activists, paying customers) is the issue here.

One possible response is repositioning of the market offering by Ryanair to place itself as a green and 'ethical' airline. However, such rebranding is a difficult and expensive process, since it requires the extensive remoulding of customer perceptions. The danger is that the outcome will be confusion in the mind of the customer and failure to impress the selected new segments. Even if it does impress the green activists, are they likely to flock to Ryanair in droves such that the expenditure on repositioning is justified by cost-benefit analysis?

Repositioning is generally regarded as a risky and expensive response to poor performance. By no measure is Ryanair performing poorly, so it is hard to see the justification for any kind of repositioning. The company is very successful according to its current model, and its newest aircraft are fuel-efficient. The Ryanair brand proposition is extremely clear. My recommendation would be not to reposition - don't fix what isn't broken.

According to Michael O'Leary: 'While the minister has been talking nonsense we have been spending in excess of $10bn (€7.6bn) over the last five years in buying the most modern, youngest and fuel-efficient fleet of Boeing aircraft that exists in Europe and in so doing reduced per passenger fuel consumption by 45% and CO2 emissions by 50% per seat.'

5 Workbook practice questions

> This section includes practice questions to help you prepare for the exam. Answers are not provided, as often at this level there is no single correct answer. However, BPP plan to provide guidance relevant to some of these questions on the web (in 2013). Check www.bpp.com/lm/cimresources for further details.

5.1 SWOT and Ansoff

(a) Explain the process of conducting a SWOT analysis and discuss the importance of the SWOT analysis for marketing planning purposes. **(10 marks)**

(b) Explain how the Ansoff matrix could be used in helping to identify and select marketing strategies for an organisation of your choice. **(10 marks)**

5.2 Decline stage marketing

A publisher identifies that one of their products – a special interest photography magazine – is in the decline stage of its product life cycle after enjoying many years with high sales in a growth market. You have been asked to submit a report that:

(a) Discusses the likely characteristics of the magazine during the decline stage. **(10 marks)**
(b) Advises the company on the marketing mix strategy to be adopted for the magazine. **(10 marks)**

5.3 Approaches to pricing

A car manufacturer has identified that the current pricing policy is not effective.

(a) Explain
    (i)   the financial approach, and
    (ii)   the economist's approach to pricing decisions. **(10 marks)**

(b) Discuss how the marketer's approach to pricing differs from both of the above approaches. **(10 marks)**

(c)   Explain what impact the Internet may have had on pricing decisions for a car manufacturer. **(5 marks)**

5.4 Targeting and positioning: airline

As a marketing assistant for an international airline company, you have been asked to produce a **report** which:

(a)   Explains the principle of targeting and positioning, and outlines the advantages that it can deliver to your company.   **(10 marks)**

(b)   Identifies and illustrates, with examples, **six** characteristics of customers that can be used to segment the international airline market.   **(10 marks)**

5.5 Marketing and corporate strategy

What are the characteristics of strategic decisions at the corporate and marketing level, and how can a strategic perspective at the marketing level be developed?   **(20 marks)**

5.6 Financial analysis

As a newly appointed marketing manager with profit responsibility for a wide range of consumer durables that are sold though several types of distribution network, draft a memorandum to the financial director explaining types of financial analysis you require and how the results will be used.   **(20 marks)**

5.7 Mission and objectives

Illustrate the essential differences between an organisation's mission, policies, aims and objectives.

(15 marks)

5.8 Discount oriented competitor

A major bank has declared that it is going to enter an already very competitive motor insurance market and offer highly competitive prices to customers. You have been asked to provide a briefing paper advising a financial services company, which is a well established direct insurer, on the options open to them when faced by this new discount orientated competitor.   **(20 marks)**

5.9 Information about competitors

Your company's markets are becoming increasingly competitive. Explain how you would develop an effective competitive information system in these circumstances, the nature of the inputs that the system would require and how the outputs from the system might be used to improve the strategic marketing process.   **(20 marks)**

5.10 Bowland Carpets

Bowland Carpets Ltd is a major producer of carpets within the UK. The company was taken over by its present parent company, Universal Carpet Inc, in 1995. Universal Carpet is a giant, vertically integrated carpet manufacturing and retailing business, based within the USA but with interests all over the world.

Bowland Carpets operates within the UK in various market segments, including the high value contract and industrial carpeting area – hotels and office blocks etc. – and in the domestic (household) market. Within the latter, the choice is reasonably wide ranging from luxury carpets down to the cheaper products. Industrial and contract carpets contribute 25% of Bowland Carpets' total annual turnover which is currently £80 million. During the early 1990s the turnover of the company was growing at 8% per annum, but since 1997 sales have dropped by 5% per annum in real terms.

Bowland Carpets has been known traditionally as a producer of high quality carpets, but at competitive prices. It has a powerful brand name, and it has been able to protect this by producing the cheaper, lower quality products under a secondary brand name. It has also maintained a good relationship with the many carpet distributors throughout the UK, particularly the mainstream retail organisations.

The recent decline in carpet sales, partly recession induced, has worried the US parent company. It has recognised that the increasing concentration within the European carpet-manufacturing sector has led to aggressive competition within a low growth industry. It does not believe that overseas sales growth by Bowland Carpets is an attractive proposition as this would compete with other Universal Carpet companies. It does, however, consider that vertical integration into retailing (as already practised within the USA) is a serious option. This would give the UK company increased control over its sales and reduce its exposure to competition. The president of the parent company has asked Jeremy Smiles, managing director of Bowland Carpets, to address this issue and provide guidance to the US board of directors. Funding does not appear to be a major issue at this time as the parent company has large cash reserves on its balance sheet.

Required

To what extent do the distinctive competences of Bowland Carpets conform to the key success factors required for the proposed strategy change? **(20 marks)**

5.11 The Lens Shop

The Lens Shop Ltd (TLS) is a camera retailer based in the UK. It currently has 15 outlets based in the major centres of population.

There are two types of retailers selling cameras in the UK. On the one hand, there are stores that sell a limited range of cameras amongst a range of other electrical and domestic appliances. These are mainly large department stores and electrical retailers that sell computers, hi-fis, televisions and cameras. Then there are specialist camera stores that only sell photographic products. TLS is one of the major retailers in this more specialist camera sector.

As well as selling the majority of the leading brands, TLS also is the largest and most well established outlet for discontinued products, used by all the distributors to clear their shelves of old product lines. These products are discounted heavily by TLS. TLS are able to buy in bulk and as a result can negotiate extra discounts.

All TLS stores are small and are located on less expensive secondary sites in the city centre but away from the main, high rent, shopping centre locations. As the outlets are small, they need less stock for display purposes and have very limited stock room space. Management feel that small stores have a better atmosphere, are less formal and hectic, yet friendly.

TLS's main promotional vehicle is a colour catalogue, which is described as '16 great pages of bargains'. This is very much seen as a fun brochure promoting products in a positive light-hearted way by mixing illustrations, technical details and humour. The catalogue is distributed in a number of ways: to people coming into the stores, from racks outside the store, by freephone telephone hotline and via a database of past customers. Media advertising is also used. Typically, camera magazines will carry a five-page advertisement, which highlights current bargains and often contains a promotional voucher for discounts or free accessories.

Prices are highly competitive, often discounted below recommended retail levels. The customer is provided with a price guarantee that TLS will beat any current local price by £10 for a similar brand of camera. TLS also offer a three-year warranty at an extremely low price. Additionally, their warranty offers a unique guaranteed buy-back service for customers wishing to upgrade their photographic equipment. Management sees this as a genuine customer service, which will hopefully encourage customer loyalty. All goods are subject to a 14-day exchange.

The company also aims to give high levels of customer service. Members of staff have a high degree of product knowledge. Sales assistants are particularly helpful, advising on the best purchases for any given budget. Staff are also happy to demonstrate the equipment. Selections of recent reviews from camera magazines are also available in the store to provide further information to customers.

To maintain required levels of customer service all customers are given a short questionnaire and asked to return them to the Managing Directors of TLS by freepost. The Managing Director reviews all comments relating to customer service, and responds where appropriate.

Required

As the new Marketing Manager for TLS you have been asked to identify and explain the sources of the organisation's competitive advantage and whether their current position is sustainable. **(15 marks)**

5.12 Empire Chemicals

Empire Chemicals is one of the UK's largest companies with several divisions including paints, pharmaceuticals, bulk chemicals, and agrochemicals such as fertiliser. Empire Chemicals detected three years ago that the financial performance of its paints business was deteriorating. Profits were steady, but its return on capital was falling. Mr Matthew Black, the main board director responsible for paints, reacted quickly to cut costs. Despite a 6% fall in turnover in the last two years, profits of the division have been rising, albeit modestly. Unfortunately, not all the divisions had such foresight. Empire's total profits are falling sharply. Mr Scott Wallace, a chemical industry analyst, says that Empire neglected to keep its costs under control in the past. Management controls are 'relatively undisciplined'. This is the legacy of a complicated management structure, which divided financial responsibilities confusingly between territorial and business managers. The autonomy of divisional heads is considerable.

Sir Denis Mack Smith created Empire's first globally organised businesses – first a world-wide pharmaceuticals operation and then, in 1984, a global agrochemical division. An increasing number of Empire's operations were set up to operate on an international basis, to meet the trans-national requirements of so many of its clients. However, Sir Denis did not streamline the organisation completely.

A parallel power structure, based on geography rather than products, has been kept in place. Because Empire is ahead of the pack in running divisions on a global basis, analysts believe that it must be careful not to neglect the differing needs of European, Japanese and US purchasers. A director points out that only 20% of Empire's business is purely domestic, but the Chairman and main board executives spend a disproportionate amount of time on UK matters.

Empire itself has long considered itself virtually bid-proof. It is one of the UK's biggest employers with 53,700 employees in Britain and it spends some 70% of its £679m R&D budget at home. However Cobb Holdings plc has purchased a stake with a view to a takeover.

Despite years of efforts by Empire to refashion itself, which did make it more international and produced a gush of profits when times were good, the company is still spread thinly across an array of separate products and markets ranging from research-intensive products to PVC (which goes to make plastic buckets). Empire has many products, in many different markets.

The company's embattled chairman, Sir Henry Sanderson has had to eat his words about the company being recession-proof. 'When I suggested that I saw no return to the dark days of recession, I was clearly wrong,' he acknowledges.

Required

To what extent do you think strategic planning has succeeded or failed at Empire Chemicals? Briefly outline an alternative model. **(20 marks)**

5.13 Feasibility study

Organisational background

SJM is a long-established retail organisation operating 227 supermarkets nationally. It is a listed company which has expanded over its 60-year history. The company has attained distinctive competitive advantage by stocking and selling only high-quality products. SJM plc has enjoyed profitable trading and now ranks as one of the leading retailers in the country. It has not been affected by restructuring of the retailing industry and its Board is intent on maintaining the company's independence.

The Board of the company has set a clear aim of achieving profitability with efficient consumption of resources, whilst maintaining the sale of high-quality goods and delivering a courteous and efficient service to customers. This overall aim has been incorporated within the mission statement and forms a central part of the company's promotional advertising.

Financial characteristics of the company

The following information is supplied in respect of SJM plc for the last financial year.

	£million
Turnover	2,400
Earnings attributable to ordinary shareholders	220

There were 1,200 million ordinary shares in issue at the end of the last financial year and the company's share price was £4.03.

SJM plc has established that its cost of capital is 12% per annum. Over the last year, the company's share price has varied between £3.30 and £4.05. SJM plc paid a dividend of £0.12 (12 pence) per share in the last financial year and has achieved steady dividend growth of 8.4% per annum over the last five years.

'Out-of-town' stores

The company has recognised that its customers are increasingly using personal transport and value the convenience of 'out-of-town' locations. 'Out-of-town' means that a store is located on a city's fringes rather than in the centre. The object of building stores in such a location is to provide customers with easier access to shopping facilities as this is often difficult within the busy city environment. Typical of the out-of-town location is a large car parking facility and good public transport links.

SJM plc established a plan five years ago to build a number of out-of-town superstores to an original design near four major cities. The first of these superstores has now been in operation for one year. The other superstores are in various stages of completion.

SJM has followed its competitors in developing out-of-town sites and is considering a partnership initiative with another retailer whose merchandise would not be a competitive threat. This would involve joint development of superstores on out-of-town sites. The only commitment to this initiative by SJM plc, so far, is a feasibility study of a single joint project with the other retailer. This will be completed before entering any contractual obligations.

The superstore strategy

SJM aims to provide a satisfactory return to its shareholders. The superstore which is already operational has achieved a high level of profitability in its first year of operation. The company has also experienced a simultaneous reduction in return obtained from other stores which it operates within the vicinity of the superstore. SJM plc is aware of growing governmental concern at the impact out-of-town developments are having on city centre retailing. These two factors have caused the company planners to pause before approving any other out-of-town developments. In addition, public transport provision has been established to service the operational superstore, but the transport providers are now objecting that there is insufficient demand to maintain frequent services as most customers travel to and from the site by car.

Superstore developments

The superstore developments are all built to a standard specification which comprises 40,000 square metres. The life of the project is fifteen years. Typically, the development takes place over a three-year period from planning stage to final commissioning. Each superstore is assumed, for investment appraisal purposes, to have a life of 12 years following completion. The cost of the first superstore development was £25 million with approximately 20% being incurred in the first year. The remaining costs are split evenly over the second and third years. Included within these costs was £500,000 for architects' fees which have reduced by half in subsequent developments. The architects' fees can be assumed to fall due for payment in direct proportion to the building costs.

The superstore developments are targeted to achieve a net cash inflow of £250 per square metre per annum from the commencement of operations. Experience has shown that the first superstore has achieved this target during the first year of operation. A total reduction in net cash inflow over the same period has occurred in other SJM plc stores which trade within the surrounding areas. This has been calculated as having the effect of reducing the superstore net cash inflow by £40 per square metre per annum.

Each superstore is assumed to have a net residual value of zero. All cashflows can be assumed to occur at the end of the year to which they relate. The cashflows and discount rate are in real terms (ie they have been adjusted for inflation).

Financial appraisal of the first superstore

		£'000	Discount factor @ 12%	Present value £'000
Cost of development				
1	(£25m) 20%	5,000	0.893	(4,465)
2	(£25m – £5m) 50%	10,000	0.797	(7,970)
3	(£25m – £25m) 50%	10,000	0.712	(7,120)
Total		25,000		(19,555)

	£'000	Cumulative discount factor	Present value £'000
Revenue over 12 years			
Gross £250 – 40,000 sq metres	10,000		
Less £40 – 40,000 sq metres	(1,600)		
Net annual revenue per annum	8,400	4.409	37,035
Net present value			17,480

Required

(a) Comment on the financial appraisal which justified the investment in the first superstore. **(5 marks)**

(b) Identify the market opportunities and threats which SJM plc will confront if it develops more out-of-town superstores. **(7 marks)**

(c) Describe and comment on the impact of the out-of-town developments by SJM plc on each of five groups of stakeholders. **(8 marks)**

(d) Discuss whether SJM plc should pursue other out-of-town developments completely on its own or jointly with the other retailer. Pay particular attention to potential planning and operational difficulties which may arise from these initiatives. **(5 marks)**

(25 marks)

5.14 Nadir products

John Staples is the Finance Director of Nadir Products plc, a UK-based company which manufactures and sells bathroom furniture – baths, sinks and toilets – to the UK market. These products are sold through a selection of specialist shops and through larger 'do-it-yourself' stores. Customers include professional plumbers and also ordinary householders who are renovating their houses themselves. The company operates at the lower end of the market and does not have a strong reputation for service. Sales have been slowly declining whereas those of competitors have been improving. In order to encourage increased sales the Board of Directors have decided to pay senior staff a bonus if certain targets are achieved. The two main targets are based on profit levels and annual sales. Two months before the end of the financial year the Finance Director asks one of his staff to check through the orders and accounts to assess the current situation. He is informed that without a sudden improvement in sales before the year end the important sales targets will not be met and so bonuses will be adversely affected.

The Finance Director has proposed to other senior staff that this shortfall in sales can be corrected by taking one of the following decisions.

1   A significant discount can be offered to any retail outlet which takes delivery of additional products prior to the end of the financial year.

2   Scheduled orders due to be delivered at the beginning of the next financial year can be brought forward and billed before the end of this year.

3   Distributors can be told that there is a risk of price increases in the future and that it will be advisable to order early so as to circumvent this possibility.

The Board is not sure of the implications associated with such decisions.

Required

(a)   As a consultant, prepare a report for the Board of Nadir Products examining the commercial and ethical implications associated with each of the proposed options mentioned above.   **(10 marks)**

(b)   Assess the significance of the corporate social responsibility model for Nadir Products.   **(15 marks)**

(25 marks)

5.15 Supermarket tyres

Rubbing shoulders with the supermarkets

You are the marketing assistant for Rubber Dubber Ltd. Your company currently manufactures rubber tyres for some of the leading branded tyre companies around the world. However, you have been approached by a leading worldwide supermarket chain that is keen to open up fast-fit tyre fitting outlets on many of its petrol forecourts, which are strategically placed alongside its supermarkets. The supermarket chain wants to know if you are interested in manufacturing tyres on its behalf, to be sold in its new outlets. Your tyres would be sold under the supermarket brand. On the face of it, this seems a wonderful opportunity for Rubber Dubber Ltd. It would however be in direct competition with the other leading brands and you are sceptical about their competitive reaction. You need to make a recommendation on this problem, with reasons, to your Board of Directors, based on the following information.

The following extract is reproduced by kind permission of Mintel International Group Ltd.

The UK tyres market has been affected by a global over-supply of tyres since 1999, causing cutbacks in manufacturing worldwide and in the UK. Other factors such as rising oil prices (in 2000 in particular) and the depreciation of the euro have also contributed to the weakening demand in the tyres market. Sales of replacement tyres in the UK stood at an estimated 28.8 million units in 2001, an increase of 26% since 1996. Volume sales have grown only steadily in the last few years, due in part to improvements in tyre technology

that have led to the introduction of longer-lasting tyres that need replacing less often. The tyres market looks set to face an uncertain future in the short-to-medium term.

Table 2.1   Market for replacement types, by value and volume, 2001–05. Source: Mintel

Year	Million Units	£ Million
2001	28.8	1,210
2002	30.0	1,235
2003	31.0	1,259
2004	31.9	1,274
2005	32.7	1,279

One of the main problems facing the UK tyre industry in the last few years has been the continued rise in imports of cheap tyre brands from Asia Pacific and, to a lesser extent, from Eastern Europe. Most consumers view tyres as distress purchases, so are not necessarily inspired to spend heavily on new tyres when required. Research also shows an apparent apathy towards tyre maintenance.

As the tyres market becomes increasingly cut-throat and the global economy slows down, the dominance of the stronger and larger manufacturers has increased. The leading manufacturers of car tyres in the UK are Michelin, Goodyear/Dunlop and Continental. Along with the likes of Pirelli and Bridgestone/Firestone, these companies tend to supply most of the major car manufacturers (see Table 2.2). The increasing consolidation of the global tyres market can be evidenced by the trend for major manufacturers to enter into agreements with other companies to maximise profits.

* Includes Dunlop/Sumitomo

Table 2.2   Manufacturers' shares in the replacement tyres market. Source: Mintel

Manufacturers	1999 Million Units	%	2001 (est) Million Units	%	% Change 1999–2001
Michelin	5.7	21	6.0	21	+5.3
Goodyear*	5.4	20	5.8	20	+7.4
Continental	3.8	14	4.3	15	+13.2
Pirelli	2.2	8	2.3	8	+4.5
Bridgestone/Firestone	0.8	3	0.6	2	-25.0
Avon	0.5	2	0.3	1	-40.0
Total top six	18.4	68	19.3	67	+4.9
Others	8.6	32	9.5	33	+10.5
Total	**27.0**	**100**	**28.8**	**100**	**+6.7**

Despite some bad publicity in the consumer press about service in some fast-fit chains, the replacement tyres market is still dominated by fast-fit outlets, both chains and independent dealers (see Table 2.3). The smaller local chains tend to be perceived to offer more personal service by some consumers and so they usually get better results in any survey of service standards at fast-fit outlets. That said, the Ford-owned Kwik-Fit chain is still the largest fast-fit retail chain. Many of the fast-fit chains now offer extensive mobile units to provide services such as tyre replacement to motorists who are on the road, at work or at home.

	Million units	%
Fast-fit chains	14.4	50
Independent fast-fit chains	9.2	32
Car dealers and garages	4.3	15
Others (including supermarkets)	0.9	3
Total	**28.8**	**100**

Continued growth in new car sales and increase in the size of the UK car park (ie the total number of cars in use on the roads) should, at the very least, sustain demand for replacement tyres over the next five years even at a time when many economic indicators are very pessimistic. It is now relatively easy and cheap to take a car across the English Channel and so this may become an increasingly attractive alternative for business and leisure travellers. Finally, the increased affluence of UK consumers has meant that more people own newer cars and premium or performance cars. The popularity of 4WD (4-Wheel Drive) vehicles and people carriers or multi-purpose vehicles (MPVs) has also boosted the tyres market in that tyres for these categories tend to be more expensive than for standard cars.

Required

Write a formal report to your marketing manager, which outlines the arguments for and against Rubber Dubber Ltd entering into a business relationship with the supermarket chain.   **(25 marks)**

5.16 Crispers and dippers

Leaner times...

You are the new product development manager at Crispers and Dippers Ltd, and two days ago your marketing director called you in to discuss the following article in the marketing press:

'The trends which have encouraged a snacking culture – less formal eating habits, time pressures and so on – will continue to be influential in coming years. However, savoury snacks products come from various food sectors, eg confectionery, biscuits, cakes, dried fruit, cheese, yoghurt/fromage frais and meat. Manufacturers in these areas have become more skilful at targeting the snacker with products that meet specific snacking needs and occasions.'

This means that the competitive environment for crisps and savoury snacks has grown tougher and that it will be harder to achieve growth. Advertising and promotion, and New Product Development (NPD) will be necessary just to maintain market size.

'To achieve real growth, the industry will need to come up with products and formats that address particular needs. This is especially the case for crisps, where penetration is so high that it will be difficult to attract new consumers in large numbers. Penetration for savoury snacks is lower and in principle has more growth potential, although there has been a slowdown over the last two years, so this will not automatically translate into higher sales growth.' (*Mintel, 2011*)

Crispers and Dippers Ltd manufacture crisps and so this article has greatly concerned your marketing director. She wants you to prepare a formal report where you will make recommendations as to new product development opportunities for Crispers and Dippers Ltd and their subsequent promotion. Use the following data to form the basis of your report. She has asked for recommendations.

The following extract is reproduced by kind permission of Mintel International Group Ltd (May 2001).

The total value of the market for crisps and savoury snacks grew by 2.5% in 2000 to reach almost £2.2 billion.

Table 2.4 Crisps and snacks market, 2001–05. Source: Mintel

	Crisps £ million	Snacks £ million	Total £ million
2001	1,219	1,000	2,219
2002	1,262	1,011	2,274
2003	1,303	1,029	2,332
2004	1,311	1,038	2,349
2005	1,346	1,055	2,401

Crisps enjoy a very high penetration level. Strong branding and promotional activity has fought off the challenge from own-label (see Table 2.5).

Table 2.5 Trends in main monitored media advertising expenditure on crisps and snacks by manufacturer (Fictional)

	1998 £ million	1999 £ million	2000 £ million	2001 £ million	2002 £ million	% change 2001-2002
Walkers Snack Foods	9.26	9.46	10.83	14.99	12.31	-17.9
McVitie's	1.71	3.73	2.95	2.73	5.84	+113.9
P&G	2.77	6.03	6.71	5.47	4.96	-9.3
KP Foods	6.74	2.01	2.87	2.17	3.39	+56.2
Golden Wonder	2.61	1.38	2.82	1.45	3.13	+115.9
Jacob's	0.63	0.81	1.18	0.36	2.52	+600.0
Others	0.99	1.52	3.14	0.63	3..15	+400.0
Total	**24.71**	**24.94**	**30.50**	**27.80**	**35.30**	**+27.0**

Advertising and on-pack promotions are very important in this market, where consumers often buy on impulse, or have to choose between quite similar products. However, it is also a very price-conscious market, where consumers tend to buy in bulk. Therefore a lot of promotion centres on cutting prices or providing extra product, eg buy-one-get-one-free, extra product free, an extra number in multipacks and so on. Most crisp and snack suppliers now have one or more websites to provide information about the company and its products and to provide interactive fun for children and teenagers for products aimed at them which feature games and special offers.

The industry is well aware of the need to have the right format for the right occasion, eg 25g bags in multi-packs for the children's lunchbox sector and 175g re-sealable sharing bags for consumption in front of the television. The conventional wisdom has been that savoury snacks have more potential for NPD than crisps. However, the boundary between crisps and savoury snacks is becoming more blurred in marketing terms. Crisp-like savoury snacks have been in evidence for many years, most significantly with Pringles.

Suppliers in the market realise that they have lagged behind other impulse sectors in terms of NPD and are paying more attention to varying products in other ways other than just the flavour. Products such as Doritos 3Ds, Hula Hoops XL, and Wotsit Wafflers and Weenies vary size and texture, and point a new way forward in NPD. Hula Hoops OX is designed to bring in young adult consumers, ie those who are older than the 12-16 year old target market for Hula Hoops.

The low-fat sector is arguably an ill-defined sector and needs further NPD before it can really take off (see Table 2.6, which shows how people responded in a recent survey, when asked the question. What kind of crisps have you bought in the last three months?). This sector has suffered as a result of products finding it hard to combine low-fat content with satisfactory taste. The most successful products, Walkers Lites and Pringles Right, are low fat compared with their standard equivalent, however they have taken sales from their parent brands.

Table 2.6   Purchase of key types of crisps in last three months, by demographic sub-group (Fictional)

	Branded Crisps %	Own-label Crisps %	Low-fat Crisps %	Any Crisps %
All	64	21	14	75
Men	64	20	13	72
Women	64	22	16	78

Required

Using relevant information from the data prepare a formal report for your Marketing Manager. Your report should make proposals for new product development opportunities for Crispers and Dippers Ltd. You should also indicate who your target audience would be for these new opportunities. **(25 marks)**

5.17 Washing detergents and laundry aids

The following extract is printed with kind permission of Mintel.

Demand for washing detergents and laundry aids is driven by a number of factors, the key ones being ownership of washing machines (determining the type of detergents needed), household size, which influences the pack sizes purchased, and product innovation. The first of these factors is showing a long-term increase, while the second (i.e. household size) is in long-term decline, suggesting an increase in demand for automatic washing powders in smaller pack sizes.

Increasingly, competitive pressure in the laundry section in supermarkets is driving the development of new product propositions and categories. The market requires heavy investment in research and development, with the time from drawing board and test lab to market being cut dramatically. New Product Development activity creates interest and awareness, as well as giving consumers improved products and reasons for trading up.

In the detergents sector, the most recent innovation has been the introduction of liquid capsules (liquid detergent encapsulated in gel capsules which dissolve in water), bringing the convenience of a unit dose of detergent to liquid users.

As Table 2.7 shows, UK retail sales of clothes-washing detergents have seen a recent decline. Continuous investment in new product development is reducing the speed of decline to a certain extent, but manufacturers are increasingly pushing product innovation in order to maintain their market positions, which are under intense pressure.

The Chartered Institute of Marketing

Table 2.7   UK retail sales of clothes-washing detergents, by value, 2000-2010. Source: Mintel

Year	Sales £ Million
2000	985
2001	1,123
2002	1,166
2003	1,173
2004	1,122
2005	1,105
2006	1,126
2007	1,152
2008	1,157
2009	(Est.) 1,170
2010	(Est.) 1,183

Mintel estimates that the market for washing detergents was worth just over £1.1 billion in 2005, representing a growth of an estimated 12% since 2000. The prime reasons behind the growth have been the strong performance of branded products and in particular, consumers trading up to more expensive formulations and tablet formats.

The supply structure for clothes-washing detergents is heavily concentrated, dominated by just a handful of manufacturers dominating, as Table 2.8 shows.

Table 2.8   Brand shares of clothes-washing detergents manufacturers, by value, 2004–06. Source: Mintel

	2004	2006
Brand	**%**	**%**
P&G	51	50
Lever Fabergé	35	35
Own brands/Other labels	14	15
Total	100	100

High levels of brand awareness are typical of this market. Advertising and promotion are therefore key features driving the market for detergent and laundry aids. The major players spend substantial sums on advertising, with prime-time national TV commercials an important element in targeting a mass-market audience.

Reports suggest that the media mix is changing, however, which has led to a fall in advertising spend. Press and media campaigns now form key elements in media selection, while sponsorship is being seized upon to improve brand awareness. Radio, press and the Internet – all of which are more lifestyle-specific and targeted to particular consumer groups – are likely to feature prominently in the future.

Required

You are a marketing assistant for a company which manufactures washing powder outside the UK, and which now wishes to enter the UK market. While doing some research for this new market development opportunity, you came across this Mintel article.

Being selective with your data, write a formal report to your marketing manager. Summarise the key factors that are highlighted in the article. Then make recommendations as to whether your company should move into the UK washing powder market, fully supporting your recommendations from the facts available.

(25 marks)

Answers to these Practice questions are not provided, as often at this level there is no single correct answer. However, BPP plan to provide guidance relevant to some of these questions on the web (in 2013). Check www.bpp.com/lm/cimresources for further details.

CHAPTER 3

Marketing leadership and planning

Topic list

1 Unit overview and syllabus

The purpose of this unit is to enable students to develop effective high-level marketing strategies relating to an organisation's corporate and business strategic intent in the short, medium-and long-terms. Students should be able to analyse the corporate strategy, determine a range of high-level marketing and relationship strategies, and demonstrate how these strategies will deliver an organisation's desire for growth and expansion and its changing stance on CSR, ethics and key strategic decisions.

In order to deliver effective, innovative and creative marketing plans, students must recognise the need to deliver sophisticated change management programmes, designed to enable an organisation to be increasingly flexible and responsive in meeting the changing requirements of the market place, balanced against the requirements of the corporate strategy. This will require students to consider the reasons for change and the types of change management plans that should be put in place.

This unit is designed to provide a detailed understanding of the major issues in developing a relevant, agile and flexible market-oriented organisation, which can respond to a dynamic and changeable market environment. Students should demonstrate a detailed understanding of the issues concerning the degree of influential leadership required to execute such change within an organisation, both from the top down and from the bottom up. This will require a thorough understanding of the resources required to implement change within an organisation and to establish the level of competence and capability required to deliver an organisation's value proposition to its markets.

1.1 Overarching learning outcomes

By the end of this unit, students should be able to:

- Critically evaluate the links from the corporate strategy to the marketing strategy and ways of delivering effectively an organisation's corporate mission and vision.

- Develop an organisation's competitive and sustainable marketing and relationship strategies to achieve the organisation's strategic intent and deliver its value proposition.

- Develop strategic and operational marketing plans at organisational level using synergistic planning processes, taking account of different planning frameworks (cross-functional and board level contribution) and ensuring they are within the resource capabilities of an organisation.

- Determine the most appropriate organisational structures for market-oriented organisations and changing organisations, while evaluating the resource implications and requirements.

- Develop sustainable competitive advantage through suitable approaches to leadership and innovation.

- Assess the link between change programmes, marketing activities and shareholder value, show how these can contribute to an organisation's ongoing success, and evaluate the concepts of power, trust and commitment in the context of negotiating change with key stakeholders.

1.2 The approach

The approach you take to your assignment must involve critical analysis and strategic thinking. We will remind you of the syllabus in a moment, of which the three main areas are:

- Delivering Marketing Strategies
- Strategic Marketing Planning
- Market-led Strategic Change

As you move up the ladder of success, based on your studies and your CIM qualifications, you will be moving into a much more strategic role. The Marketing Leadership and Planning assignment reflects this. In your response to the assignment brief, you would do well to bear in mind the comments made regarding 'postgraduateness' in Chapter 1.

Let's look now a specific example. The main themes of the December 2011/March 2012 assignment brief were **innovation and learning**, with a particular focus on **organisational flexibility, responsiveness, agility and 'leanness'.** This last term – also associated with 'Toyotism' – very much in vogue in current business circles, implies the elimination (as wasteful) of anything that does not contribute value.

These are not tactical issues and involve a high-level strategic approach to marketing effectiveness. As always, in marketing, we are concerned with value-creation that is appropriate for the selected Target Group and consequently the creation of shareholder value. This was the thinking behind the March 2012 assessment, as well as the wish to ensure that candidates made decisions that were appropriately justified and evaluated. The Senior Examiner's report (available on the Learning Zone website) makes reference to the need for the correct level and depth of analysis to be undertaken before any recommendations are made. This is particularly important when looking to develop a culture of innovation and learning.

The final part of the March 2012 paper was on Leadership. Candidates were asked to produce a discussion paper that critically evaluated the skills necessary to leadership in order for the chosen strategy to be successful.

The CIM Magic Formula for this level tells us that the accent is on Application (30% of the mark) and Evaluation (45%), with only 15% for Concept (knowledge of theories and models) and, as always, 10% for presentation. The report on the March 2012 contains the following insights.

Concept: in this case, candidates needed to identify the key relevant theoretical principles associated with agility, 'leanness', responsiveness and a sustainable, competitive position, ensuring that they were correctly evaluated and applied to their chosen organisation.

Application: candidates always need to be able to critically analyse the key areas of knowledge, applying them as most appropriate.

Evaluation: the important thing here is to describe the decision-making process and the rationale behind it and therefore to demonstrate how key recommendations were made, using previous analysis to underpin the thinking. The examiner refers the need for originality and insight into complex areas.

Presentation: as usual, candidates are expected to communicate in a professional as well as academic fashion. Would you present this work to your Board of Directors (actually, it is probably a good idea to present it formally to your superior, in the organisation).

Syllabus Part 1 – Delivering marketing strategies

SECTION 1 – Developing and delivering an organisation's vision and mission
(weighting 30%, of this part)

1.1.1	Critically analyse how to create a clear, simple, reality-based vision for an organisation and its stakeholders:
	▪ Identifying strategic intent
	▪ Creating a unique image of the organisation for the future
	▪ The balance of inspiration versus capability and capacity
	▪ Enlisting stakeholders in future possibilities
	▪ Balancing internal and external constraints on the vision for the future
	▪ Organisation's aspirations and purpose
1.1.2	Critically evaluate the importance of mission statements in communicating an organisation's strategic vision and identity, including:
	▪ Purpose, feelings and direction
	▪ Basis of objectives
	▪ Basis for strategy
	▪ Focal point for stakeholders
	▪ Values of the organisation, including moral, ethical and sustainability positioning
1.1.3	Identify distinctive competences of the organisation and how they can be leveraged to achieve an organisation's mission:
	▪ Distinctive essence of the organisation
	▪ Market and business definition
	▪ Intended positioning in the marketplace
	▪ Role of contribution and identification of future intent
1.1.4	Examine the different approaches to the strategic process:
	▪ Emergent, Logical incrementalism (Mintzberg/Quinn)
	▪ Deliberate (Kotler, Wilson and Gilligan, McDonald)

SECTION 2 – Developing marketing strategies and the value proposition
(weighting 70% of this part)

1.2.1	Determine an organisation's value proposition through analysis of an organisation's vision, mission and corporate objectives: ■ Market definition ■ Setting strategic objectives ■ Price/value and proposition
1.2.2	Utilising the strategic audit, develop and present corporate strategies that are creative, customer-focused, innovative and competitive for a variety of contexts, incorporating relevant investment decisions and business cases which meet corporate objectives: ■ Product/market strategies ■ Growth strategies ■ Competitive strategies ■ Global and channel strategies ■ Brand and positioning strategies ■ CRM strategies
1.2.3	Critically evaluate the marketing strategy process, utilising the three key areas/levels in marketing strategy development: ■ Core strategy ■ Creation of competitive positioning (market targets, differential advantage and cost leadership) ■ Control

Part 2 – Strategic marketing planning

SECTION 1 – Strategic marketing plans (weighting 30% of this part)

2.1.1	Critically evaluate the concept of strategic marketing planning as a tool to deliver an organisation's value proposition: ■ Efficacy of formalised marketing planning ■ The specification of sustainable competitive advantage and marketing planning and its contribution to commercial success and to delivering the organisation's value proposition ■ Preparedness to meet change and implement market-focused orientation across the organisation ■ Contextualisation of marketing planning in a corporate framework (McDonald, 2007)
2.1.2	Analyse the corporate objectives and translate into overarching marketing objectives to support giving direction to a marketing plan: ■ The interactive process – balancing an organisation's ambitions with knowledge from individual business units ■ Relevant marketing objectives to enhance the attainment of the firm's ability to satisfy customers and foster innovation ■ From corporate objectives to setting a balanced array of marketing objectives that cover marketing and financial aspects

2.1.3	Assess the variables facing an organisation in order to assess the impact of the future corporate and marketing objectives against its current competences, resource capacity and financial positioning:
	■ Analyse key areas within an organisation:
	– Market share
	– Innovation
	– Resource
	– Productivity
	– Social aspects and profit
	– Alternative measures of success eg, for NFP
	■ Core competences:
	– Potential access
	– Significant contribution
	– Difficulty for competitors to copy
	■ Auditing resources:
	– Technical resources
	– Financial standing
	– Managerial skills
	– Information systems
	■ Ansoff matrix and Gap Analysis
2.1.4	Make clear recommendations that determine either changes in the strategy or further resource requirements to support the delivery of the strategic marketing plan:
	■ Resource audit
	■ Core competences for the attainment of a successful marketing plan
	■ Marketing audit to underpin the marketing plan
2.1.5	Develop marketing plans utilising corporate planning frameworks to deliver an organisation's strategies and meet corporate objectives:
	■ Planning typologies
	■ Marketing design and implementation of planning systems
	■ Integration of the marketing planning process with organisation's overall strategy and objectives (to include: corporate and strategic issues, competition, industry, SWOT, business environment [PEST], marketing objectives, strategy, monitoring evaluation)
2.1.6	Critically evaluate why marketing plans can fail:
	■ Design and implementation issues
	■ Gaining management support
	■ Separation of operational planning from strategic planning
	■ Integration of marketing planning into a total corporate planning system

SECTION 2 – Assessing and utilising organisational resources and assets
(weighting 40% of this part)

2.2.1	Assess an organisation's structure and critically evaluate its appropriateness to align and deliver its strategy and fulfil its vision:
	■ Centralisation versus decentralisation
	■ Lines of authority and communications
	■ Committees, teams, taskforces required
	■ Organisational life phases

2.2.2	Critically evaluate existing systems and processes and identify future needs in line with an organisation's strategy requirements:
	
	   ■ Budget setting
	   ■ Planning systems
	   ■ Accounting systems
	   ■ Information management and flows

2.2.3	Assess the competency of an organisation's workforce in order to establish future capability and capacity requirements:
	
	   ■ Skills, knowledge and expertise
	   ■ Quality and fit
	   ■ Employee expectations
	   ■ Attitudes

SECTION 3 – Monitoring and measuring marketing (weighting 30% of this part)

2.3.1	Critically evaluate the concepts of adaptability, efficiency and effectiveness as means of measuring the success or otherwise of marketing strategies for a range of organisational sectors:
	
	   ■ Efficiency/effectiveness matrix in measuring longevity of marketing strategies (McDonald, 2007)
	   ■ Tactical versus strategic orientation

2.3.2	Critically evaluate and use quantitative techniques for evaluating business and marketing performance and delivery of the marketing strategy, including:
	
	   ■ Brand equity and brand value
	   ■ Shareholder value analysis
	   ■ Benchmarking analysis
	   ■ Comparative assessments with previous strategies and budgetary control techniques

2.3.3	Measure financial returns achieved as a result of specific investment decisions and compare them to the original investment appraisal or business case:
	
	   ■ Historic decisions informing current decision-making
	   ■ Short-term versus long-term
	   ■ Linkages between strategic and financial appraisal from manager's own perspective (in a strategic management context – Grundy and Johnson 1993 BJM)

2.3.4	Propose and critically evaluate the development of sustainable marketing strategies and ethics, and analyse the value generated by these strategies to the organisation's overall strategy:
	
	   ■ Investment in sustainable marketing strategies
	   ■ Developing appropriate messages to stakeholders and shareholders
	   ■ Sustainable product development strategies and communication methods to influence consumer behaviour in a long-term sustainable context

2.3.5	Assess the value that the marketing proposition has generated and how it can contribute to shareholder value:
	
	   ■ Value-based planning models
	   ■ Creation of additional value
	   ■ Role of marketing due diligence

Part 3 – Market-led strategic change

SECTION 1 – Strategic marketing plans (weighting 30% of this part)

3.1.1	Critically evaluate and identify the methods for measuring successful and effective leadership strategies in determining and defining an organisation's strategic focus and intent:
	
	■ Different leadership theories in achieving strategic focus:
	
	      – Trait approach/Behaviour approach
	      – Power/influence approach
	      – Situational approach
	      – Integrative approach

3.1.2	Critically evaluate a range of approaches to successful leadership of the organisation and of the marketing function: ■ Characteristics of a successful leader ■ Characteristics of followers ■ Characteristics of the situation • Relating and integrating the primary types of leadership approaches in order to ensure successful and effective leadership strategies ■ Ethics of leaders
3.1.3	Critically evaluate and analyse the dominant leadership paradigms: ■ Classical/Visionary/Transactional/Organic ■ Organisational considerations according to different leadership paradigms
3.1.4	Critically evaluate the concept of power and influence in promoting a coherent philosophy regarding sources of power and how it can be exercised in the organisation: ■ Influence processes (Kelman proposed three different types of influence processes – instrumental compliance, internalisation and personal identification) ■ Different types of power according to their source (French and Raven, 1959) ■ Control over information power ■ Dichotomy between position power and personal power (Bass 1960, Etzioni 1961)
3.1.5	Critically evaluate the concept of bi-cultural leadership in developing capabilities effectively within new sub-cultures and across boundaries: ■ Examine how leaders create an organisational climate that encourages a healthy balance between collaboration and competition • Which encourages risk-taking and risk assessment and which is boundary-less
3.1.6	Explore ways of developing thought leadership within the organisation to assist in the development of a culture of innovation and learning, including: ■ Keeping stakeholders connected ■ Engaging and expediting learning ■ Developing a learning organisation ■ Investing in knowledge capital through knowledge management ■ Maintaining knowledge of innovation and passing it on

3.1.7	Utilise the management team, internal resources and networks to develop tools to access key stakeholders, including: ■ Setting up steering committees ■ Establishing formal links with strategic planners and leaders ■ Establishing communities and networks with business leaders ■ Continuously seeking internal and external customer information
3.1.8	Assess your own leadership style and recommend how it can be improved and maximised to aid business thinking, working with colleagues, inspiring people and achieving goals: ■ Leadership styles (Transitional, Transformational, Traditional) ■ Group dynamics/team motivation ■ Reflective thinking and feedback ■ Different methods of measuring leadership effectiveness ■ Difficulties of measuring effectiveness of a leader

SECTION 2 – Developing a market-oriented culture (weighting 30% of this part)

3.2.1	Critically evaluate the concept of a market-oriented culture and consider the implications for an organisation in achieving it, including: ■ Customer orientation ■ Cross and inter-functional orientation ■ Competitor orientation ■ Profit orientation
3.2.2	Assess the different characteristics of culture in a broad context and evaluate the need for change to achieve true market orientation, including: ■ Values, beliefs and assumptions ■ Symbols ■ Heroes ■ Rituals ■ Culture and strategic implications ■ Organisational climate
3.2.3	Explore ways in which the organisation can go about creating and shaping a market-oriented culture: ■ Working towards common goals ■ Collective identity ■ Embracing differences and diversity ■ Common goals ■ Fostering support ■ Focus on innovation ■ Focus on performance ■ Focus on learning and development
3.2.4	Critically evaluate the concept of shared values and show how they can be effectively communicated in a market-oriented organisation: ■ Organisational values, eg CSR, sustainability ■ Cultural values ■ Ethical values ■ Economic values

The Chartered Institute of Marketing

3.2.5	Determine measures for success in transforming an organisation's culture to one of true market orientation:
	■ Externally focused organisation
	■ Market orientation matrix (Heiens 2000)
	■ Customer/Competitor focused – toward an integrated approach (Slater and Narver 1994)
	■ Market orientation and business performance

SECTION 3 – Developing and delivering organisational strategies for change
(weighting 30% of this part)

3.3.1	Assess the key drivers and pressures on organisations to change in today's dynamic marketing environment:
	■ Environmental audit
	■ Contemporary issues
	■ Global challenges
3.3.2	Critically evaluate barriers to organisational change, making recommendations of how best to overcome them:
	■ Cultural barriers to change
	■ Competency inadequacies
	■ Community barriers
	■ Personal barriers
3.3.3	Critically evaluate why organisations often avoid corporate led change, including:
	■ Public scrutiny of large corporate organisations
	■ Political/legislative reasons
	■ Union intervention
	■ Prior strategic commitments
	■ Inertia
3.3.4	Critically evaluate the different methods of change available to organisations:
	■ Incremental
	■ Discontinuous
	■ Re-engineering
3.3.5	Design a process for change, to provide insight into the level of involvement and interaction stakeholders will have in the transformation of an organisation and its market orientation, including consideration of constraints and contingencies:
	■ Surface/profound change management
	■ Organisation wide change – strategic change management
	■ Stakeholder mapping – power versus support or resistance
	■ Stakeholder personal analysis (getting inside an individual's head)
	■ The nature of opposition (knowing your 'enemies' in change)
	■ The nature of support (knowing your allies in change)
	■ Measuring the impact of change
3.3.6	Prepare a change plan for an organisation, taking into account the need for appropriate resources, capabilities, skills and motivations for its execution:
	■ HR policy – recruitment, training, job definition and roles, rewards and incentives, relationships and hierarchies
	■ Customer/competitor relations
	■ Cross-function and inter-departmental relations
	■ Innovation
	■ Integrating internal and external pressures
	■ Monitoring and measuring success

2 The assignment brief

The assignment brief is the document that sets out everything you need to know to complete your work-based project assignment:

- The submission date: when your project must be submitted (and when results will be released) and what is required.

- A rubric or set of instructions in regard to the marks available, the maximum word count for the project, and the documentation which should accompany the assignment.

- Guidance Notes on teaching, project preparation and assessment.

- A Mark Scheme, with a breakdown of the marks available for each of the Assessment Criteria – cross-referenced to the CIM Magic Formula (discussed in Chapter 1).

- Guidance on tackling the assignment, specifically related to the tasks and topics of the given Project Brief.

2.1 The exemplar assignment brief

In this section, we reproduce the Exemplar (Specimen) Work Based Assignment material published by the CIM, and provide some guidance to:

- Suggest how such material can be interpreted, for the best sense of what it is that examiners are really looking for.

- Highlight key instructions which should form part of your 'compliance checklist' when planning, compiling and checking your assignment work.

- Indicate how the format illustrated by the Exemplar could be used to target a range of syllabus themes, topics and types of task.

In some instances, we have made slight alterations to the Exemplar Assignment Brief as published by the CIM, to correct typographical errors, or to reflect the formula that may be subsequently adopted in the 'live' Assignment Briefs.

2.2 Rubric (front page instructions)

Specimen Work-Based Assignment

Assessment

- All tasks within the chosen project brief are compulsory
- 100% of the marks available for this paper
- Maximum word count – 8,000 words

Word count

Candidates must adhere to the word count stated. No marks will be allocated for information contained in appendices, unless explicitly stated within the assignment brief. Appendices should be used for supporting information only. CIM reserves the right to return **unmarked** any assignment that exceeds the stated word count or contains, in the opinion of the examiner, excessive appendices.

Word count is obviously extremely important, and further guidelines on how to adhere to it are given below. Although there is less guidance on the use of appendices, it is worth bearing some key principles in mind:

- The Project Brief will clearly state what appendices are *required* (and at what length) as part of the assignment. One appendix will certainly contain your 'organisation background': a brief overview of the

organisation, which is the focus of your project. Another, may be the detailed findings of a stakeholder audit or analysis, for example.

- It would also be appropriate to use appendices to contain your list of references (sources referred to in the body of the report) and bibliography (books and other secondary sources consulted in preparing the report).

- Other appendices may be used to supply supporting information (such as research findings) or documentation (such as a stakeholder feedback questionnaire), a summary of which should be included in the main body of the report.

- Appendices are not included in the word count, but *do not* use them to try to squeeze in material for which you do not have 'room' in the body of your report. You will not gain marks for the material – and 'excessive appendices' may disqualify your assignment altogether. (Examiners have long seen through the 'hide the extra 1,000 words in an appendix' ploy.)

Documentation

Candidates must complete the required declaration front sheet and ensure that they are registered with CIM as a student member – and for this assignment – by the required deadline. Tutors are also required to sign the declaration front sheet, stating that, to the best of their knowledge, the work that the candidate is submitting is their own.

2.3 Guidance notes

Context

The assignment should be based on the candidate's organisation, or an organisation of their choice, selected with tutor advice. A brief overview of the organisation chosen, including legal classification, product or service offered, target market and structure, up to a maximum of two A4 sides, should be included in the appendix. This information should not be included as part of the word count and no marks will be allocated to this section. Candidates should ensure that sensitive data from the chosen organisation is not included or ensure the anonymity of the organisation used within the assignment. Each assignment must be completed individually, not as part of a group.

Assessment criteria

The assignment briefing documents include the marking scheme and guidance notes which are designed to indicate to the candidate the types of information and format that are required. The marking scheme should not replace any briefing that is usually undertaken by the unit tutor. It is important that, when assignments are issued, discussions take place between the group and tutor to clarify their understanding of the assignment brief and what is required.

Tutor guidance to candidates

Each candidate should receive a minimum of 60 minutes tutorial time per unit scheduled at key periods throughout the undertaking. Tutors should be prepared to offer advice to candidates regarding the tasks, particularly with regard to the organisation they choose to use.

Tutors can give feedback on **one** draft of an assignment and/or answer specific subject-related questions from a candidate related to their assignment. Tutors should not return a completed assignment to the candidate for improvement. Evidence of a centre doing this will result in the assignment being sent back unmarked.

Word count

Candidates must comply with the recommended word count, within a margin of 10%. Any assignments that exceed this will be penalised by candidates forfeiting the marks for presentation for each individual task where the word count has exceeded the +10% margin. Work that grossly exceeds the recommended word count will be returned unmarked and candidates will be asked to complete and submit a new assignment. Where a candidate's work has exceeded the word count it will be reviewed by the senior examiner.

Word count excludes the index (if used), headings, information contained within references, bibliography and appendices. Candidates should present their work professionally using tables and diagrams to support and/or illustrate the text. Tables and diagrams should be included as appendices but must be referred to within the main body of the text for marks to be awarded. If candidates use tables to present their answer in the main body of the text, the words used will be counted and the rules relating to word count, as indicated above, will apply.

When an assignment task requires candidates to produce presentation slides, with supporting notes, the word count applies to the supporting notes only. The maximum number of slides indicated on the assignment brief excludes the title page slide and the contents page slide.

Candidates should state the number of words that they have used at the end of each task. In addition, the total number of words used for the whole assignment must be indicated on the front cover of the assignment.

> ▶ **Assessment tip**
>
> When you start work on your assignment, make yourself a checklist of all the elements (relevant to the type of task you have been set) which are *excluded* from the word count: this will enable you to make the most of your word count and check it accurately. Aim for the maximum word count (8,000 words), rather than the +10% margin (8,800 words): this will leave you more room for editing. To give you a broad idea, this page contains about 600 words (excluding headings): your report would be a maximum of 13 pages at this level of density: more, if you include diagrams, tables and so on. Tips for managing your word count will be provided in section 5.3.
>
> Note also the helpful hints as to what the examiners expect to see in assignments: tables and diagrams to support and/or illustrate report text; and title and contents page slides as part of presentations.

Mark schemes

Mark schemes are included so that candidates are aware where the majority of the marks will come from and are therefore able to structure their work accordingly. However, CIM reserves the right to amend the mark scheme if appropriate.

Final grades

Final grades will be sent to the candidates from the CIM by the usual process in February, May, August or November, depending on when assignments were submitted for marking.

 The Chartered Institute of Marketing

Referencing and professionalism

A professional approach to work, which may account for up to 5% of the marks available, is expected from all candidates. Candidates must therefore:

- Identify and acknowledge **all** sources/methodologies/applications used. The candidate must use a Harvard referencing system to achieve this.

- Express their work in plain business English. Marks are not awarded for use of English, but a good standard of English will help candidates to express their understanding more effectively.

All work that candidates submit, as part of the CIM requirements must be expressed in their own words and incorporate their own judgements. Direct quotations from the published or unpublished work of others, including that of tutors or employers, must be appropriately referenced. Authors of images used in reports and audiovisual presentations must be acknowledged.

Plagiarism and collusion

Academic offences, including plagiarism and collusion, are treated very seriously. Plagiarism involves presenting work, excerpts, ideas or passages of another author without appropriate referencing and attribution. Collusion occurs when two or more students submit work which is so alike in ideas, content, wording and/or structure that the similarity goes beyond what might have been mere coincidence. Plagiarism and collusion are very serious offences and any candidate found to be copying another candidate's work or quoting work from another source without recognising and disclosing that source will be penalised.

It is the candidate's responsibility to make sure that he or she understands what constitutes an academic offence, and, in particular, what plagiarism and collusion are and how to avoid them. Useful guidance materials and supporting policies are available on the tutor and student websites. Tutors should also ensure that candidates are appropriately briefed about how to avoid plagiarism and collusion, especially when using electronic sources or when working in a group.

Candidates must sign the declaration front sheet with their membership number confirming that the work submitted is their own. Tutors must countersign the document to say that to the best of their knowledge the work submitted is the candidate's own. CIM reserves the right to return assignments if the necessary declaration form has not been signed.

Candidates believed to be involved in plagiarism and/or collusion will have their work looked at separately by the senior Examiner and/or another senior academic and plagiarism detection software will be used. Candidates found to be in breach of these regulations may be subject to one or more of the following: disqualification from membership; refused award of unit or qualification; disqualification from other CIM examinations/qualifications; refused the right to retake units/qualifications.

You might gather that plagiarism (claiming another person's work as your own) and collusion (working together with others on work that you claim as yours alone) are serious matters for the CIM. You would be right! However, it is important to keep this in proportion: do not be prevented from using helpful sources of information by fear that you may be suspected of plagiarism. The key points are:

- To acknowledge the source of any concepts or models you refer to (eg Greiner's Organisational Growth Model) in the text and to include the source in the list of references

- To acknowledge the source of any images you reproduce (eg photographs, drawings or diagrams) and any statistical data you use in tabular or diagrammatic form.

- To provide detailed referencing for any material that is a direct citation or quotation (using the Harvard referencing system, discussed in the Appendix of this Workbook).

- To rephrase information you have read or heard, using your own words, where possible. Do this deliberately: be aware that it is easy to slip into reproducing text, when taking notes.

When dealing with basic theoretical material, it is inevitable that people will make some of the same points on a given topic: do not tie yourself in knots trying to come up with something different – just acknowledge the source from which you have derived your understanding.

2.4 The assignment brief: Delivering the value proposition

Marketing strategy

You have been appointed to develop a new medium-term marketing strategy for your chosen organisation, with a view to maintaining your organisation's financial stability and delivering its value proposition. Your organisation may be in the profit or not-for-profit sector.

You should assume a position where you have been given strategic responsibility on behalf of the organisation to define and develop new marketing strategies to ensure continuous success in a volatile and changing world. In taking responsibility for the strategies and plans, you will need to undertake the following tasks for your own organisation, or one of your choice.

> ▶ **Assessment tip**
>
> Each Assignment Brief will start with a paragraph or two setting the context of the assignment: orienting you to its basic topic or theme. This is not just 'padding', it is important information about how the Examiner defines key terminology and sees the overall purpose of the project tasks.

Each Assignment Brief will contain a one or two-sentence role and purpose description: what you have been asked to do (eg present a report/proposal, prepare a presentation), for whom (eg your organisation's Corporate Communications Manager or Marketing Manager), and for what purpose (eg, 'that contains a set of recommendations for'…).

The Chartered Institute of Marketing

Again, this is important information, which you should use in planning your Work Based Assignment and evaluating your first draft. The format and content requirements will be set out in more detail in the task descriptions, but you *don't* get much more detail about who your target audience is – and this will be vitally important: one of the underlying tasks of the assignment is to consider the information needs of your audience.

In effect, you are being asked to treat your own organisation as if it were a case study scenario.

Task one

- Critically evaluate your organisation's existing marketing strategy, and assess how relevant it is in the current market conditions and predicted market trends.

- Recommend, with justification, the changes required to the existing marketing strategy.

> ▶ **Assessment tip**
>
> The specific terms of reference may vary from Assignment Brief to Assignment Brief: they typically comprise two or three requirements, each very clearly stated in terms of instruction/command word (evaluate, assess, recommend) and topic.

Task two

- Develop a new medium-term marketing strategy for your organisation.

- Justify how your chosen strategy will benefit the organisation in line with the organisation's corporate vision and objectives, and evaluate the impact that the strategy will have on the organisation.

Task three

- Develop a strategic marketing plan, utilising an appropriate planning framework that will successfully deliver the organisation's strategy and represent the organisation's vision and mission.

Task four

- Critically analyse the leadership skills and approach required to make the marketing strategy and marketing plan a success. In so doing, critically assess your own leadership style and evaluate your personal development needs.

- Recommend, with justification, how cultural change will be achieved and how the support of key stakeholders will be ensured.

> ▶ **Assessment tip**
>
> This is your basic checklist for planning your Work Based Assignment and evaluating each draft. You must fulfil the requirements of each of the bullet points, within your report – although you will not necessarily structure your report on a task-by-task basis: the structure of the report will be shaped by the particular issues drawn out of your audit analysis.
>
> What this part of the brief does not tell you is the relative weighting (or length of coverage) of each topic within the report. This information is provided by the Mark Scheme, which we will look at later.

Appendix

Your appendix should include a brief background to your chosen organisation, its customer base and product/service range (two sides of A4 maximum, no marks allocated).

2.4.1 Syllabus references

1.2.1, 1.2.2, 1.2.3, 2.1.1, 2.1.2, 2.1.3, 2.2.1, 2.2.2, 2.2.3, 2.2.4, 2.3.1, 2.3.2, 2.3.3, 3.1.1, 2.1.2, 3.1.3, 3.1.4, 3.1.6.

These references may appear to be of more interest to the Examiner than to you – indicating which learning outcomes the project is supposed to assess. However, it is helpful information. It will point you to: (a) what the Examiner considers appropriate underpinning content for the assignment tasks (ie which concepts, models and tools will be relevant); (b) what chapters in the Marketing Leadership and Planning Study Text will be most helpful (since the syllabus reproduced in the Text is cross-referenced to the chapters in which the content is covered).

It also provides useful reminders not to omit syllabus topics from your consideration. In the above case, for example, the inclusion of Learning Outcomes 3.1.3 and 3.1.4 should remind you to take leadership paradigms into account, and to critically evaluate the concept of power and influence in promoting a coherent philosophy regarding sources of power and how it can be exercised in the organisation.

2.4.2 Mark scheme

We have adapted the Exemplar Mark Scheme to include the CIM's Magic Formula, in the format used by the Mark Schemes of all subsequent 'live' project briefs. We have allocated marks to the Magic Formula elements based on these later Mark Schemes.

Table 3.1   Mark scheme – Delivering the value proposition

Marking Criteria	Marks available
Critically evaluate your organisation's existing marketing strategy, and assess how relevant it is in the current market conditions and predicted market trends	10
Recommend, with justification, the changes required to the existing marketing strategy	10
Develop a new medium term marketing strategy for your organisation.	10
Justify how your chosen strategy will benefit the organisation in line with the organisation's corporate vision and objectives, and evaluate the impact that the strategy will have on the organisation.	10
Develop a strategic marketing plan, utilising an appropriate planning framework that will successfully deliver the organisation's strategy and represent the organisation's vision and mission.	30
Critically analyse the leadership skills and approach required to make the marketing strategy and marketing plan a success. In so doing, critically assess your own leadership style and evaluate your personal development needs.	10
Recommend, with justification, how cultural change will be achieved and how the support of key stakeholders will be ensured.	10
Format and Presentation ■ relevance to the tasks ■ use of concepts and frameworks to support arguments, points and recommendations ■ professional tone and required format ■ appropriate use of examples to illustrate points ■ Harvard referencing	10
Total marks	**100**

The Chartered Institute of Marketing

2.4.3 Guidance on tackling the assignment

Contextual issues

Many candidates may feel quite challenged by this assignment initially because they may come from an SME or an organisation that has a strategy in place. This assessment should almost be treated as if the candidate has a blank piece of paper in which they can propose their preferred strategies and plans for the organisation as if they were in a position to do so.

The key word here is organisation, and not marketing function. This is neither a tactical nor an operational plan with functional implications, but a strategy and plan designed to move the organisation forward. The implications of this strategy and plan may be organisation wide, with significant investment and resource implications.

The aim is that candidates will be able to make an assessment of the organisation's current strategy and of how relevant it is in current market conditions with high levels of economic volatility. Candidates have been asked to consider a medium term plan. A time-frame has not been specified because what constitutes medium term will vary considerably in different sectors.

Regardless of whether an organisation is for-profit or not-for-profit, it will require a marketing strategy to bring around growth in either profit or revenue generation for investment or charitable work.

This assignment looks for an integrative approach combining the development of the organisation's strategy and the ability to take a 'whole organisation' approach.

Application and Evaluation

While this Work-Based Assignment appears to be highly applied, it is essential that candidates can show that the work they produce is built on strong foundations of theoretical principles, appropriate for the postgraduate level, and which are critically applied within a senior marketing management context.

Task one guidance

For their chosen organisation, candidates need to critically evaluate the organisation's existing marketing strategy, clearly identifying its strengths and its weaknesses. This analysis should lead to clear recommendations on changes or improvements that are required.

In their evaluation, candidates should show reliable, valid and incisive conclusions about the organisation's current strategy, and be able to argue a range of alternative strategic approaches valid to the organisation and its ability to fulfil its vision and corporate objectives. Candidates should formulate their arguments on sound theoretical principles, which are critically evaluated in the context of senior marketing management.

Task two guidance

In developing a new medium-term marketing strategy for the organisation, candidates should consider an appropriate time frame. Candidates should justify their chosen strategy, indicating why it is appropriate to the organisation, including the strategic benefits it will bring.

Consideration should also be given to how the marketing strategy will contribute to the organisation's achievement of its corporate objectives, CSR, relational and ethical objectives and ultimate vision for the future. Finally, candidates should state how the chosen strategy would impact on the organisation, including the fit with the organisation's culture.

Task three guidance

The marketing plan and planning framework should enable the delivery of the marketing strategy, in a way that represents the organisation's vision and mission. The plan should include the following:

- An assessment of the organisation's structure and its readiness for the implementation of the strategy and plans, and clear recommendations for change and improvement as part of the plan.

- An evaluation of the existing systems and processes within the organisation, with recommendations for change and improvement.

- An assessment of the organisation's current capability and capacity, with recommendations for filling the gap for implementing the new strategy.

- A critical evaluation of the budget and financial implications of your strategy, given any financial restraints that may be in place, and suggestions of ways in which your strategy may be funded, with anticipated Return on Investment (ROI), or – in a not-for-profit organisation – anticipated revenues.

- An overview of the change management requirements this strategy will involve, including a process for change that will provide insight into the level of interaction stakeholders may have and also provide the potential level of transformation required.

- Strategic measures and controls for the strategy and plan, including quantitative and qualitative techniques for measuring market performance and delivery of the marketing strategy.

Task four guidance

In order to implement the new strategy and plan, you will be expected to demonstrate significant and effective leadership, including thought leadership, in determining and defining the marketing strategy for the organisation.

You will need to provide an overview of the leadership approach required to make the strategy plan a success.

This should include a demonstration of how the strategy and plan will bring about cultural change within the organisation, to strengthen its market orientation. It is also important to demonstrate how the management team, internal resources and networks will be utilised, and how the buy-in and commitment of key stakeholders will be achieved.

In doing this, you will need to assess your own leadership style, indicating changes required to achieve the desired success of the organisation.

You should be able to show originality of thought, thought leadership, and the ability to deal with complex, dynamic issues and the unexpected.

The Chartered
Institute of Marketing

2.5 Potential assignment brief themes

Each Assignment Brief could focus on a different theme or topic, which can be applied to a wide range of organisational contexts. The Exemplar Project Brief, for ASSESSMENT plc, focused on 'Delivering The Value Proposition'.

You cannot afford to focus your study on particular areas of the syllabus, on the basis of these themes: the assignments are deliberately designed to test a wide range of learning outcomes.

This part of the syllabus incorporates all four parts of the assessment and requires students to think holistically rather than talking parts of the syllabus in isolation. The more widely and holistically you study, the better prepared you will be to tackle the Assignment Brief when it is given to you.

In the March 2012 report, the Senior Examiner very kindly provided us with a list of themes that could figure in future assessments. In fact, the last one on the list presented was – and is – the subject of the June/December 2012 assessment:

- Strategic direction and development
- Developing marketing plans
- Stakeholder value
- Monitoring and evaluating marketing decisions
- Relationship marketing
- Leading and inspiring an organisation
- Organisational culture
- Marketing strategies and the Value Proposition
- Vision and Mission (themes of June 2012 assessment)
- CSR and Sustainability (from June 2012 report)

According to the Senior Examiner: 'Marketing Planning and Leadership is a fundamental part of this unit and so will be incorporated into future assessments to a greater or lesser degree. All assessments will be focusing on corporate level and strategic issues, rather than being purely tactical in nature'.

2.5.1 Further reading

Further recommended reading is included at the end of each chapter in the BPP Study Text relation to this module. You should refer to these references to gain a deeper understanding of the models, theories and framework and their application.

In addition, there are a number of online resources you could refer. In addition to the CIM Student Area you could also refer to such websites as:

http://www.marketingsherpa.com

(a)   Under homepage 'search' add relevant syllabus key words.
(b)   Under 'Browse' then 'Topics' (a number of topics come up by Industry/Target).
(c)   SherpaBlog – a number of relevant blogs constantly changing.

http://www.businesslink.gov.uk

Select 'sales and Marketing' then 'Create your marketing strategy'.

http://www.blog.totalmarketingsolutions.co.uk

Select 'Categories' then 'Marketing Strategies'.

Under 'Categories' there are various options to choose from depending on what part of the syllabus you are exploring'.

Select 'Resource Library'.

Select 'White papers' and input the area of the syllabus you are exploring, a number of papers will be listed select the most relevant and select 'View this Content'.

2.5.2 Potential project formats and tasks

In addition, it is worth considering the range of formats and tasks that may be set for future Assignment Briefs.

Generally, the Assignment Brief published follows the Exemplar in format, requiring: (a) an evaluation of the existing marketing strategy and (b) a formal report recommending a new marketing strategy and plan.

However, there may be other formats for future Assignment Briefs, including presentation slides and supporting notes. These two formats are perhaps the most likely, since they allow for substantial work, creative thinking, professional approach, a realistic element of application and academic referencing.

In terms of tasks, the specific requirements vary according to the topic. However, some common elements have begun to emerge. Your Assignment Brief is quite likely to require:

- A brief overview of the organisation that is the subject of your Work-Based Assignment

- Some form of analysis of the existing marketing plan, including an environmental and competitive audit and so on. (The models and concepts specified by the syllabus are covered in Chapter 1, 2 and 3 of the BPP Study Text. Use this coverage as a starting point for your further reading and thinking.)

- Design and development of a medium-term marketing strategy and plan, utilising an appropriate planning framework that will successfully deliver the organisation's strategy and represent the organisation's vision and mission. (The models and concepts specified by the syllabus are covered in the BPP Study Text. Use this coverage as a starting point for your further reading and thinking.)

- Critical analysis of the leadership skills and approaches required to make the marketing strategy and marketing plan a success.

- Critical assessment of your own leadership style and evaluation of your personal development needs.

- Recommending how cultural change can be achieved and how the support of key stakeholders will be ensured.

3 Building a portfolio for your project

3.1 Why build a portfolio?

You will have noticed that you are not required to *submit* any kind of portfolio to the Institute as part of your Work-Based Assignment. So why are we suggesting that you prepare one?

- Preparing a portfolio is a helpful discipline, which requires you to collect and record a range of secondary source materials, conduct research and analysis, and file topic notes. Any or all of this may be useful groundwork, or usable material, for your project.

- It is *not* advisable to focus your studies narrowly on the Assignment theme, in the first instance: a wide-ranging and well-integrated understanding of marketing leadership and planning is required in order to interpret and tackle assignment tasks effectively. Preparing a portfolio helps you to study broadly across the syllabus, while still compiling useful material for your project.

- You may not be given access to the Assignment Brief until a late stage of your studies: building a portfolio allows you to get a head start on important groundwork such as cultural styles and leadership models, so that you can maximise the time available, later, for more focused research.

3.2 Research strategy

A key skill in the 'Concept' area of the CIM Magic Formula is the ability to 'identify relevant theoretical principles commensurate with the postgraduate level and critically apply and evaluate these within a senior marketing management context, using originality of thought' (Grade Descriptors for the Chartered Postgraduate Diploma in Marketing).

Undertaking a research strategy at the beginning of your studies – and refining it as you go along - will provide you with a range of useful material (including real-life assessment and case studies) demonstrating theories, models and framework under discussion, and the basis for a comprehensive Bibliography for your assignment. Once you have received your Assignment Brief, you can refine your research strategy further, focusing on the relevant themes and topics.

- Include a range of media: books (or chapters of books); newspaper and journal articles (printed or on-line); web sites; DVDs, videos or CD-ROMs; corporate documents, outputs (eg advertising, stakeholder communications), public statements and research reports.

- Organise your list using appropriate headings: 'general' (eg for books on Marketing Strategy) and specific topic headings (eg Vision and Mission, Marketing Planning, Cultural Styles)

- Start with your BPP Study Text and the Key Reading List titles (under the 'general' heading). As you pursue your studies, add sources from the Supplementary Reading list; Further Reading references; the CIM Knowledge Hub; your tutor's recommendations or hand-outs; and your own 'browsing'. Delete sources that, on closer inspection, lack relevance or credibility.

- When you actually consult a source:

    - Check or complete the reference details (title, author, publisher, date/edition, page numbers etc. – or web address and date posted).

    - File your notes, or a copy or print-out of the information, in a Resource File for later use.

    - Transfer the source reference to your draft Bibliography.

You might also draft an initial primary research strategy. For the development of your marketing plan, you may want to conduct a survey (using a questionnaire) or interview colleagues (one to one or in a group);, representatives of key stakeholder groups, management or other relevant parties.

Since this is a time-consuming approach, and involves other, busy people, you should save primary research until you are able to focus on the project brief: however, it will still be useful to identify potential sources of information on different topics.

3.3 Portfolio-building exercises

Your unit lecturer or tutor may suggest portfolio-building activities at different stages of your course. The following are some general suggestions for the kinds of activities you might undertake to build a project-supporting portfolio, as you work your way through the syllabus. The BPP Study Text for *Marketing Leadership and Planning* includes activities specifically designed to support portfolio-building, and we recommend that you attempt as many of these as possible during your studies: we have highlighted some of the most useful ones here.

Table 3.2   Portfolio-building

Task	Comment	Study Text guidance
Compile an on-going Research Strategy ('reading list') and Bibliography	Discussed above	*Further Reading*
Open a Resource File	File (in an organised way, indexed by topic) your study notes; excerpts from books; cuttings from magazines and newspapers; print-outs from web sites; transcripts of interviews and discussions; copies of corporate documents and so on, as you gather them. Please be aware of any copyright or confidentiality issues in storing, copying or using material.	
Collect examples of activities that support the development of a new marketing strategy in the real world, for your Resource File	This will provide illustrative examples that you can use to underpin conceptual points in your project (an important skill in the 'Application' area of the Magic Formula).	Table text
Draft your 'Organisational Background' or overview description	(If you know which organisation you will use for your project.)	
Carry out an marketing audit of your organisation	Use research techniques (brainstorming, observation, interviews, documentary evidence) to identify key stakeholders and analyse their power and interest. Draw a PEST Analysis, Stakeholder Map and/or Product/Market matrix. Write notes justifying each element of the marketing strategy. Write notes explaining (a) the organisation's vision and (b) its core competences.	
Gather evidence of your organisation's corporate vision and mission statement	Make an appraisal based upon discussions with managers and colleagues and highlight any issues: these can be followed up later, if relevant to the Assignment Brief.	Chapter 1: Activity 1
Gather evidence of your organisation's corporate vision and mission statement	Make an appraisal based upon discussions with managers and colleagues and highlight any issues: these can be followed up later, if relevant to the Assignment Brief.	Chapter 1: Activity 1

4 Tackling the Assignment Brief

4.1 Assignment technique

4.1.1 Writing an organisation background

The purpose of the organisation background or overview is:

- To brief the examiners on the context to which your project relates, so that they can judge whether your analysis and proposals are relevant and realistic in that context.

- To avoid having to describe and explain organisation details in the body of your report, which (a) would be poor communication practice in a report to your own managers and (b) would waste word count!

Read the Context section of your Assignment Brief carefully for any instructions as to required content of the overview. So far, you have been asked to include: legal classification (eg partnership, charity, private limited company, public limited company), product(s) or service(s) offers, target market and organisation structure.

4.1.2 Writing a formal report

Read the Guidance section of your Assignment Brief carefully for any instructions as to the content, structure and style of the formal report task.

4.1.3 Managing your word count

We highly recommend that you take word count into consideration at the project planning stage. Your aim is:

- To ensure that your word count is appropriately distributed across the assessment criteria, in order to achieve a good balance and maximise the available marks *and*

- To get as close to the 8,000 word limit as you can, in your first draft – to avoid frustrating and inefficient padding or pruning at the second draft stage.

Read the Guidance Notes section of your Assignment Brief carefully for any instructions as to word count. The following are some extra tips: use them if they suit your method of working.

- Start with a checklist of relevant maximum limits (in words, pages or slides) for different elements of the project, and of the *exclusions* from the word count (index, headings, diagrammatic and tabulated information, references, bibliography, appendices, title and contents page slides). Use this each time you check your count.

- Work out roughly how many words you present per average page of work, and therefore roughly how many pages your report will be: say, nine pages densely typed.

- Check the Mark Scheme for your assignment. Leaving aside the 10 marks for format and presentation, there are 90 marks available for fulfilling the task criteria. For every 10 marks, therefore, you need to allow one-ninth of the total word or page count: about 450 words, or one page. Following the maths through:

Table 3.3   Available marks/word count

Marks available for assessment criterion	Allocate:	
10	450 words	1 page
15	660 words	1 ½ pages
20	900 words	2 pages
25	1,110 words	2 ½ pages
30	1,330 words	3 pages

This is just a rough guide, but it will help with your word-count management, and ensure that you earn good marks across the assignment. (It should also be reassuring, since you do not have to write large volumes of material: the examiner is looking for quality, not quantity.)

- Do not try to 'hide' extra word count in appendices: this will not gain you marks. Use appendices only for legitimate supporting data, summarised in the body of the report.

- If you need to reduce your first-draft word count, look first for repetitions, superfluous illustrations/examples and irrelevant points: it may be easier to leave out a few short paragraphs than to cut words and phrases out of your writing style. (Unless you are a 'waffler', in which case, prune away!). Alternatively, consider whether some material might be conveyed in a diagram or table (excluding it from the word count) – with the added benefit of adding creativity and visual interest to your report.

- If you need to add to your first-draft word count, check whether you have *under*-written some parts of the task for the marks available, and add to those first. Add genuine content – *not* waffle!

- Do not forget to indicate your total word count on the front cover of your assignment.

4.2 Tackling the exemplar assignment brief - Delivering the value proposition

4.2.1 Specimen organisational background

The following overview, for the purposes of demonstration, is based on a real-life organisation, but the case study organisation and its situation are fictional.

Appendix 1: Organisation overview

The British Association of Management

The British Association of Management (BAM) is a leading UK association dedicated to the development of expertise in management practice. In addition to supporting its members, the association encourages management development, carries out research, produces a wide variety of publications on management interests, and publishes the official members' magazine, *Management Monthly*. It has over 40,000 members in the UK and several thousand more around the world.

Vision and Mission

BAM's vision is to be the UK's most effective association for managers through raising standards in management practice. Its mission is to:

- Help businesses improve efficiency and effectiveness
- Share the latest insights and standards in management development
- Reward and recognise best practice in management

Background

BAM was established in 1969 by a prominent industrialist and entrepreneur, Sir Harold James, with the endorsement of the UK Government to ensure that UK industry could raise its performance of business through good management. By 1993, over 500 organisations had signed up to the BAM Charter promoting good standards of management practice. It believes that strong business performance and the delivery of public services depends on high quality management and leadership.

It is committed to encouraging and supporting the lifelong development of managers and to raising the standards of management performance.

Foundation and legal form

BAM was incorporated as a not-for-profit company, limited by guarantee (with members acting as guarantors, rather than shareholders). It is defined as a voluntary organisation, set up for charitable purposes ('the

 The Chartered Institute of Marketing

advancement of management practice', as defined by the *Charities Act 2006*), and is registered as a charity in England, Wales and Scotland.

BAM Enterprises Limited is a wholly owned subsidiary of the Association, offering commercial services in management development and publishing.

The Association has over 40,000 members, and enjoys the patronage of HRH Prince Andrew.

Competition

BAM has been dominant in its field for the past forty years. However with the emergence of online business networking communities it has found itself under increasing pressure from more entrepreneurial competitors who are stealing market share with a proposition more in line with 21st century thinking. These competitors offer a different pricing structure that ensures that managers around the world pay a membership fee appropriate to their purchasing power, and with an offering that is more relevant to their needs.

Products and services

The core aims of the Association are to help its members tackle the management challenges it faces on a daily basis by raising the standard of management in the UK. It is committed to helping people become better managers and organisations develop better managers.

It does this through a wide range of products and services, from practical management checklists to tailored training and qualifications. BAM produces research on the latest 'hot' management issues, provide a vast array of useful information through the library, as well as offering consultancy services and career information.

Its primary form of revenue is through membership. Choosing to join the BAM brings with it professional recognition and a wide range of support services that will aid a manager's development throughout their career.

It helps organisations maximise the potential of their management teams by running in-house and bespoke management training for a range of clients. It enables organisations of all sizes, from all sectors to realise fully the potential of its managers and leaders.

In recent years, the Association has undertaken more policy work to shape public perceptions of management and raise the credibility of the management profession. It plays a key role in spreading the highest standards of management practice and promoting awareness of leading issues through the media.

Recognising the international development of business, it has begun to establish links with overseas management associations, universities and training partners to broaden and strengthen its reputation and brand awareness in international markets. However, it's UK-centric approach and commercial model is hindering progress in this area.

Organisation structure

The Association employs a core staff of around 40 people with many volunteers (eg as branch committee officers) and contractors (eg on training projects and event management). The permanent management structure of the Association can be summarised as follows.

Figure 3.1   Management structure of the Association

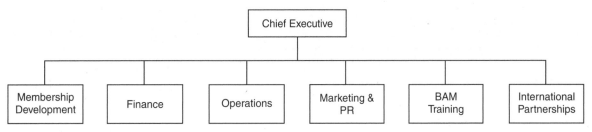

Governance

The Association is governed by a Board of Trustees, made up of President, Immediate Past President, Chief Executive, six elected members (three academics and three from practice). As well as fulfilling the statutory requirements as Trustees of the charity, the Board considers and approves the strategic objectives of the Institute and monitors their implementation. The Board is supported by a number of Committees, which consider policy and corporate governance issues. Broadly speaking, policy is decided by the Board of Trustees and implemented by the Management Team.

▶ **Assessment tip**

A few things to notice about our specimen overview:

- It occupies a maximum of two A4 pages.

- It gives a broad overview, but because of the technical nature of the organisation's activities, it focuses in more detail on some areas (in order to brief the examiner) than another organisation might require. When writing your overview, you might have more room for a survey of organisation culture, key suppliers/distributors/allies, business processes, future plans and so on: see some of the other Case Study organisation backgrounds in this Workbook for examples. Be selective in the information you include.

- It covers the details required by the Assignment Brief – but not in a formulaic way: it meets the needs required by the examiner and draws practically on appropriate sections of the syllabus. Be flexible in your thinking, and remember to contextualise your material to the particular organisation you are looking at.

- It includes deliberately elements, which will support later discussion of relationship marketing (the theme of the Assignment Brief): mentioning a range of stakeholder audiences, the potential for an international element, and a number of potential RM activities (including fundraising and lobbying).

- It references sources of information (which would be cited in the References appendix of the report).

This task is worth doing well. Although it earns no marks, it may be the first thing the assessor reads, and therefore needs to create a good first impression of your clarity, judgement and professionalism.

▶ **Assessment tip**

If you haven't already done so, now would be a good time to attempt a first draft of your Organisation Background. If you haven't chosen an organisation for your project, draft an overview of any organisation that interests you: still good practice. Consider what sorts of information are relevant – and at what depth, in order for you to keep to two pages and still give a good overview briefing.

Exemplar assignment brief: Task one

Critically evaluate your organisation's existing marketing strategy, and assess how relevant it is in the current market conditions and predicted market trends. Recommend, with justification, the changes required to the existing marketing strategy.

Note

We are not going to present a full formal report, the contents of which will be largely irrelevant to your actual Assignment Brief. We will simply highlight how you might go about tackling each component of the task set in the Exemplar Assignment Brief, with reference to the specimen organisation and Organisation Background, and provide note-form specimen points for an answer.

The Chartered Institute of Marketing

Assess the organisation's marketing strategy by taking into account internal and external organisation factors, for example:

- The organisation's capability, resources, strategic intent and stakeholder expectations.

- Consider the overall marketing strategy process, evaluating the different factors involved in marketing strategy development and relating it back to the organisation.

- Identify and justify strategic choices and options.

- Justify how you are going to measure the plan and why that form of measurement is most appropriate in the context of the organisation.

- Critique the current measurement strategies and recommend revised or more appropriate forms of measurement.

This task requires you to undertake a marketing audit. This can be achieved through various methodologies and techniques

- A survey of the market, conducted with members, clients and other key stakeholders. This can be achieved through a variety of research methods:

  - Secondary Research – undertake a competitive analysis by assessing other membership associations and training organisations both in UK and overseas. This could involve benchmarking product performance and evaluating BAM product and service range versus others. This can be undertaken by visiting their websites, obtaining their brochures and catalogues and visiting their conferences and events.

  - Primary Research – in-depth interviews and focus groups with members and clients; personal interviews with internal management such as Operations Manager and Marketing and PR Manager; personal interviews with volunteers who are co-opted to local Branches.

- Secondary research on marketing strategy theory, analytical tools and methodologies.

- Environmental Analysis – out of this, you can produce a PESTLE Analysis and a Porter Five Force Analysis to gain an understanding of the macro and micro-environment and the current and future trends and issues that can have an impact on the future success of the organisation. What might have worked for today might not work tomorrow. Changes in economic conditions may have an impact on the wants and needs of members in terms of the support they require (ie support during a recession will be different) and revenue projections.

- SWOT Analysis – it is essential that a review is undertaken of the organisation, its capabilities and resources. It will be essential to have personal interviews with colleagues in HR to ensure that BAM has the resources required to meet future needs. For example, if the home market is experiencing decline or zero growth it might be necessary to divert resources to international development.

- Product Portfolio Review – ideally, an organisation should have a portfolio of products and services whose life cycles overlap in order to guarantee continuity of income and growth potential. Undertake a review of each area of activity its contribution to total revenue and the overall success of BAM. Review whether there is room for growth for each product, whether it is in decline and needs rejuvenating, whether further investment is required in its development or whether it needs to be discontinued.

- Measurement and Evaluation – assess the appropriateness of the performance and monitoring framework and associated measures and make suggestions to the strength and weaknesses of these, highlighting any recommendations as required

- Management Process Review – review the process by which the marketing plan and strategy is developed, reviewed and agreed and whether this needs to be amended and adapted in light of future trends

> **▶ Assessment tip**
>
> There is other content you could include here, but you have to be careful not to pre-empt your content for following sections: eg, by developing a new marketing strategy for the organisation or evaluating the impact that the strategy will have on the organisation. This content should be useable for other types of organisation, except that you might include 'customers' in a more explicit way in your examples. The actual context of the Assessment Brief may prove to be challenging if you work for an organisation that already has a strategy written. If this is the case, assess the current strategy and develop it according to external changing market factors and also the internal context.

Exemplar assignment brief: Task two

Develop a new medium term marketing strategy for your organisation.

Justify how your chosen strategy will benefit the organisation in line with the organisation's corporate vision and objectives, and evaluate the impact that the strategy will have on the organisation.

> **▶ Assessment tip**
>
> This requires you to assess the development of a marketing strategy by taking into account internal and external organisational factors, such as, the organisation's capability, resources, strategic intent and stakeholder expectations. It will mean identifying the distinctive competences of the organisation and how those link to the corporate vision. This requires practical application as well as sound justifications. Any decisions made need a rationale that is appropriately backed up by the relevant organisational information. Do not just repeat your Strategic Marketing Audit findings verbatim. Do not forget to cross-reference your summary to your Appendix where relevant, clearly numbered.

- A Strategic Audit was undertaken to identify the key issues facing BAM. There will be no need to repeat the details of the Strategic Audit but a good marketing strategy makes good use of the analysis undertaken. Whilst one would never argue that you should over-analyse everything, you do need to ensure that any marketing strategy is based on as clear an understanding of the market environment as possible.

- A medium-term marketing strategy is typically 2-5 years for an organisation. This is the case for BAM. Do consider the state of the environment. Medium-term marketing strategies are all well and good in a stable market environment as long as the short term is taken care of. BAM is under competitive pressure and it would be wise to consider these issues, sooner rather than later.

 The Chartered Institute of Marketing

- The marketing strategy requires clear objectives and a focus, in line with the organisation's mission and goals. BAM has a clear mission statement. You should have considered in the Strategic Audit whether or not the mission is still relevant or whether it needs to be refined.

- It is recommended in light of the competitive pressures that the mission be revisited to undertake a more international perspective and use more modern language. Accordingly the recommended and revised vision is:

  'BAM's vision is to be the worldwide professional development association for the management community ensuring that businesses can create world class managers wherever they are in the world'.

- This revised mission will need to be discussed with colleagues across the organisation. Clearly, this new direction is a response to market pressures and, whilst a knee-jerk reaction cannot be taken, senior management must act swiftly to support this and demonstrate their support for it. This will be discussed in Task 3 so there is no need to go into detail here.

- The most powerful way to prevail in global competition and particularly in challenging and uncertain times is to be clear about the roots of competitive advantage. The organisations to emulate are those that are adept at reinventing themselves, inventing new markets, quickly entering emerging markets and dramatically shifting purchasing patterns in established markets. In the long-run, competitiveness derives from an ability to build, at lower total cost and more speedily than competitors, the core competencies that spawn unanticipated products.

- The real sources of competitive advantage are found in management's ability to consolidate organisation-wide technologies, production skills, knowledge and learning into competencies that enable the organisation to adapt quickly to emerging opportunities and fulfil the organisation's mission.

- One of the key impacts of this new direction will be on the capabilities and resources required. BAM has a number of distinctive competences some of which will serve it well in the future. Few organisations are likely to build world leadership in more than five or six fundamental competences.

- There seems to be a gap that will need to be filled between the capabilities they have now and the capabilities they require. It would be useful to make this clear in your Assignment Brief.

Table 3.4 Current and required competences

Current Competences	Required Competence
Forty years of reputation and experience in serving UK market	International expertise to ensure relevance and resonance with overseas markets
UK-based expertise in training and professional development	Worldwide understanding of the needs of business and their managers
Good knowledge of publishing	Digital and online publishing expertise to create new content and ensure wider distribution
Good partnership with universities and associations	Collaborative/partnership based arrangements
Emerging international recognition	International marketing expertise
'Royal' endorsement	Global recognition and endorsement
Experienced management team	New ideas and practices to compete effectively with private sector and drive the international agenda

- Considering the future direction of the organisation requires a review or restatement of intent of the organisation's competitive strategy. Michael Porter (1985) suggests there are three generic strategies for competitive advantage.

  - Cost leadership means being the lowest-cost producer in the industry as a whole.

- Differentiation is the exploitation of a product or service, which the industry as a whole believes to be unique.

- Focus involves a restriction of activities to only part of the market (a segment) through:

- Providing goods and/or services at lower cost to that segment (cost-focus)

- Providing a differentiated product or service to that segment (differentiation-focus)

- BAM has been following a differentiation-focus – it has commanded a premium position within the management sector. You need to question whether this is the correct strategy to pursue going forward. With a substantial UK based overhead, it is difficult to move away from this position and it might seem foolish to do so. BAM therefore has to work harder at communicating its position in the marketplace and the benefits it provides to its members.

- It is important to state the benefits of continuing to pursue this policy – however any good strategist also considers the risks of pursuing a desired strategy. A good leader will then identify ways to minimise the risks, for example:

Table 3.5   Advantages and disadvantages of differentiation focus

Advantages of differentiation focus for BAM	Disadvantages of differentiation focus for BAM	Risk Minimisation
Has achieved strong brand loyalty over the years and become known for its reputation	New competitors are breaking into the sector and creating their own loyal customers	Focus on identifying the needs and priorities of the most loyal members, reward their loyalty and retain them
Ordinarily, potential members have had no comparable substitute	Differentiation can be created by new entrants too, particularly those that begin to obtain some transaction in the marketplace and advocates of their own	Reinforce the benefits of being a member of BAM – for the member, for the employer. Identify new market/product opportunities that can be implemented relatively quickly at low cost but are in line with the mission and are value-adding
Strong capabilities in training and development can be leveraged and built upon	Costly to maintain these capabilities and need to continually require evaluation and investment in new areas of management practice	Need to evaluate new opportunities opening up in online publishing and distance/online education given the global and online nature of the competition. Does BAM compete, acquire or divest?

So, assuming BAM is not going to move away from its competitive strategy of differentiation-focus you will need to consider how it is going to defend as well as grow its market. BAM is still (and for the time being at least) the market leader. Therefore, attack is the best form of defence. However, there is a recognition that it needs to adapt to the emerging pressures.

The Chartered Institute of Marketing

Figure 3.2: Ansoff

Ansoff's product-market growth matrix

	Existing products	*New products*
Existing markets	**Market penetration strategy** 1 More purchasing and usage from existing customers 2 Gain customers from competitors 3 Convert non-users into users (where both are in same market segment)	**Product development strategy** 1 Product modification via new features 2 Different quality levels 3 'New' product
New markets	**Market penetration strategy** 1 New market segments 2 New distribution channels 3 New geographic areas eg exports	**Diversification strategy** 1 Organic growth 2 Joint ventures 3 Mergers 4 Acquisition/take-over

- Market Penetration Strategy (example)

    – Reduce likelihood of lapsed membership by incentivising loyalty (member-get-member schemes), encouraging early-bird take up of training programmes and events and so on.

    – Communicate to members the benefits of being a member of BAM.

- Market Development Strategy

    – Identify new market sectors (eg student membership).
    – Identify overseas markets (eg overseas markets, which are growing).

- Product Development Strategy

    – Create new distance learning qualification.
    – Create E-books, podcasts and webcasts.

- Diversification

    – Create new membership association, aiming at different business discipline.

- Each of the identified options will need to be evaluated in terms of cost/revenue benefits to the organisation. An initial screening might be undertaken to assess those that have the most/least perceived impact on the success of the organisation. You will also need to assess the best available method of implementing the alternatives. For example, in expanding overseas there are a number of alternative routes to market like franchising, joint-venturing, or establishing full-owned overseas operations.

- There may also be products that BAM has that are in need of renewal or discontinuing. For example, a programme or workshop may no longer be relevant to its members or is out-of-date. It is essential that such products are identified and that action is taken quickly in order that they do not become an unnecessary drain on resources.

- Clearly a reassessment of the organisation's activities is required in light of the revised mission for BAM.

BAM is governed by a Board of Trustees, made up of President, Immediate Past President, Chief Executive, six elected members (three academics and three from practice). As well as fulfilling the statutory requirements as Trustees of the charity, the Board considers and approves the strategic objectives of the Institute and monitors their implementation. The Board is supported by a number of Committees, which consider policy and corporate governance issues. Policy is broadly decided by the Board of Trustees and implemented by the Management Team.

BAM has many of the characteristics associated with a role culture. This is typical of hierarchies in which the job and pace within an organisation are well defined. Personal power is derived from the job and its position within the hierarchy. It encourages introversion and bureaucracy and can be inflexible and slow to change.

If it is to realise the opportunities available to it a fundamental shift in culture will be required. We recommend that it move towards a task culture where success is judged on outcomes. It will require a more flexible and dynamic culture, drawing on the task in hand and the skills and capabilities of individuals in the organisation regardless of their place in the hierarchy.

It is recognised that such a fundamental shift cannot be achieved overnight and that any success will only be achieved with the full support and commitment of the senior management team.

Exemplar assignment brief: Task three

Develop a strategic marketing plan, utilising an appropriate planning framework that will successfully deliver the organisation's strategy and represent the organisation's vision and mission.

The Chartered
Institute of Marketing

The marketing plan and planning framework should enable the delivery of the marketing strategy, in a way that represents the organisation's vision and mission. The plan should include all or some of the following aspects:

- An assessment of the organisation's structure and its readiness for the implementation of the strategy and plans, and clear recommendations for change and improvement as part of the plan.

- An evaluation of the existing systems and processes within the organisation, with recommendations for change and improvement.

- An assessment of the organisation's current capability and capacity, with recommendations for filling the gap for implementing the new strategy.

- A critical evaluation of the budget and financial implications of your strategy, given any financial restraints that may be in place, and suggestions of ways in which your strategy may be funded, with anticipated Return on Investment (ROI), or – in a not-for-profit organisation – anticipated revenues.

- An overview of the change management requirements this strategy will involve, including a process for change that will provide insight into the level of interaction stakeholders may have and also provide the potential level of transformation required.

- Strategic measures and controls for the strategy and plan, including quantitative and qualitative techniques for measuring market performance and delivery of the marketing strategy.

What follows is an outline template of a strategic marketing plan for BAM. You will need to ensure that your own strategic marketing plan reflects more closely the requirements of your own organisation under investigation.

Strategic Marketing Plan: British Association of Management

Vision

'BAM's vision is to be the worldwide professional development association for the management community ensuring that businesses can create world class managers wherever they are in the world'.

It will achieve this through:

- **Helping managers with their career**
- **Raising standards in management practice, worldwide**

Given the change in the competitive environment, it needs to provide a more global offering in supporting managers wherever they work in the world, by enabling them to be more knowledgeable, capable and better networked.

Overview of the market

In this section, you need to include a commentary of the market situation. You should draw on the analysis that you developed in Task 1 and the strategy that you recommended in Task 2. There is no need to repeat the same information here.

Marketing objectives

The objectives are goals that the organisation would like to attain during the plan's term, in this case, the next 3-5 years. Most organisations use strategic marketing plans to support a direction of growth. BAM has recognised that it needs to see a change in direction and therefore the marketing objectives will reflect this business requirement.

When an organisation chooses growth as a strategy its marketing plan will need to define objectives in financial terms, such as achieving higher turnover or profit, or – in the case of charitable or not-for-profit organisations –

an improvement in gross margin. Many organisations may also define societal objectives, for example, performance in areas of social responsibility and stakeholder relations.

It might be useful to set out marketing objectives in three categories: financial, marketing and societal objectives.

BAM's direction is to retain its existing membership and acquire new members and clients through international expansion and product development. Based on the mission and direction, we have formulated the following primary objectives for our strategic marketing plan:

Financial objectives

- Achieve increases in turnover of 10%2010-2012
- Increase gross margin by 15% by 2012

Marketing objectives

- Reduce likelihood of lapsed membership by incentivising loyalty, thereby reducing 'churn' by 20% by 2012.

- Increase acquisition of members by 10% per year within the next three years.

- Expand into at least five new overseas markets by 2012.

- Create a new distance learning qualification with a UK university, to be validated by September 2012.

- Create a new range of E-books on management practice, which will be launched by September 2012.

Societal objectives

- Create a socially sustainable and commercially viable pricing strategy that enables mangers around the world access to our services on a fair and equitable basis.

- Implement a scholarship scheme to support one student per year over the next three years from a developing country to attend a management programme in the UK.

> ▶ **Assessment tip**
>
> Note that we have attempted to draft SMART objectives. Marketing must increasingly ensure that its activities can be measured and justified in terms of their return on investment and contribution to the success of the organisation.

Product strategy

BAM needs to update the training and development solutions it can offer in management education. The way in which executive education is being delivered is changing. People are learning in different ways. This will involve the development of a new work-based management qualification and the development of a series of E-books, podcasts and webcasts to support continuing professional development.

In order to establish a go-forward strategy BAM will undertake further research and development to identify the opportunities that exist. In order to recommend the desired product range we will undertake a new product development process to identify, assess, recommend and develop the desired products.

The Chartered
Institute of Marketing

The following table demonstrates the key desired elements of BAM's proposed product strategy:

Table 3.6   BAM's proposed product strategy

Product mix	Work-based management qualification
Product life cycle	Provide a new qualification that enables managers worldwide to gain the necessary skills and capabilities in line with best practice.
New product development	Develop a globally transferable qualification that is recognised by employers worldwide as the 'gold standard' in management practice.
Quality and Performance	Developed by world leading academics and practitioners in management practice, capable of being studied anywhere in the world.
Features and benefits	Capable of being studied online, at own pace.
Brand	Emphasises the BAM brand and recognises key brand endorsers and partners to ensure credibility.
Design and packaging	Build on BAM identity, create global appeal through use of imagery.
Product life cycle	Provide a new qualification that enables managers worldwide to gain the necessary skills and capabilities in line with best practice.

Pricing strategy

BAM has a number of pricing objectives in relation to the new qualification:

- **Financial**

    Contribution to a 5% improvement in total organisation turnover within three years of operation

    Achieve turnover of £200,000 in its first full year of operation

- **Marketing**

  Encouraging take-up in early stages through providing 10% introductory discount to existing clients and members

- **Social**

  Establishing a global pricing system to ensure that maximum take-up can be achieved, regardless of purchasing power

In the early stages, we will price this product aggressively to ensure that we achieve early take-up and acceptance by the market. We will offer introductory prices to our existing clients and members.

In order to retain our premium positioning and ensure the product remains competitive and attractive in the market we will adopt a market penetration strategy, designed to achieve widespread coverage and take-up in the early stages. This must be balanced with our desire to ensure that the qualification is priced commensurate with a world class management qualification.

Promotional strategy

> ▶ **Assessment tip**
>
> In developing your promotional strategy, you should consider an integrated marketing communications strategy that focuses on specific target audiences. You will need to consider the appropriate objectives, budgets and resources required and how you intend to monitor and evaluate results. Outline at least one promotional programme. Below we consider the outline of the promotional strategy for BAM in relation to its new qualification.

Given the start-up and investment costs associated with the new management qualification, BAM's promotional strategy will rely less on paid-for advertising and more on PR, direct marketing, personal selling and digital marketing.

BAM will adopt a push strategy to ensure that our qualification is marketed and delivered through accredited training organisations. In support of this, we will provide such outlets with collateral about the qualification and educate the sales and administrative staff about the programme.

BAM will use a profile strategy to ensure that leading figures from industry that support BAM are used in the imagery that supports the promotion. Testimonials and endorsements will be used in PR to provide source credibility. Key people that have been involved in the development of the qualification will be present at qualification roadshows around the world to support and endorse the programme.

We will use direct marketing activity to drive people to the website with a separate microsite being developed which provides further information and encourages potential students to register their interest. This site will also feature podcasts with key people involved in its development and a PDF brochure and application form so that people can download further information.

Potential students will be directed towards a dedicated email and telephone number where a dedicated customer service team will respond to enquiries. Online ordering of materials will be facilitated through the website.

In line with BAM's policy, a budget will be allocated based upon achieving the required objectives. Accordingly, we will allocate 10% of expected turnover towards marketing expenditure.

> ▶ **Assessment tip**
>
> We have given as broad a range of suggestions as we can. You may want to be more selective at greater depth. You may also want to add an Appendix with examples of campaigns used by similar organisations.

The Chartered
Institute of Marketing

Internal marketing strategy

Since BAM is undertaking a process of change, it must develop processes that motivate the wider BAM team to improve its performance. The following measures can be considered:

- Emphasise value gained in return for extra effort: new skills, greater contribution to the cause, new opportunities;

- Add rewards/incentives (without incurring cost): eg Marketer of the Month award (for most new students registered on the qualification);

- Address identified concerns: emphasise support for initiative, tolerance of learning curve; re-define perceptions of marketing as 'helping students to maximise their personal development';

- Follow up with on-the-job coaching programme and mentoring system (using more confident/experienced staff to support others in the 'new BAM world');

- Set up dedicated intranet pages for BAM staff: on-going guidance and tips, news of staff awards, blogs by award winners, discussion boards for good news and advice swapping;

- Gather and feed back performance being achieved against objective on a monthly basis, so that staff can monitor and celebrate their financial contribution.

Marketing programme

In this section, you could include a time-plan of activities by calendar month to demonstrate what activity is being undertaken, when and by whom. If you are undertaking a number of projects, it might be easier to develop a programme of activity for each to begin with, then to identify opportunities for integration and compile one time-plan.

Measuring the strategic marketing plan

- Data should also be monitored on conversion of enquiries to students; numbers of new memberships and numbers of upgraded memberships contained in responses. The member database should also be able to provide the membership figures and changes for stated periods;

- Similar measurement can be made through response/enquiry telephone lines (using computer telephony integration to input caller details direct to database) and web site traffic and analytics (carried out automatically by the software);

- It would also be helpful to run inquiry tests as new marketing initiatives are introduced, to identify the success of particular tools or promotions, and progress over the period of the plan, in terms of number of inquiries and cost per inquiry;

- Media exposure and share of voice measurement as well as recall and recognition testing, are already utilised by BAM to cover advertising and PR, but these are of less relevance, as the marketing objective is focused on conversion to students and memberships

- Internal financial analysis should track measurable increases in membership fees / programme fees over time. This will be a useful measure, to demonstrate that incentives (and other costs of motivating sales) are 'profitable' in terms of increasing overall contribution through memberships

- Qualitative measures might also be helpful in order to support the further refinement of the plan. For example, feedback forms, survey questionnaires (administered by post or on-line) and perhaps focus group interviews (with new corporate or educational members) could be used to analyse: what attracted new members to the membership proposition or students to the qualification; where/how they signed up; whether they feel membership is good value for money; what their experience of BAM membership has been like for them so far, and so on.

- Over time, BAM will also have information in regard to retention rates (percentage of new members remaining after one year) and defection rates (percentage of members not renewing after one year, two years etc). This will also help to indicate whether the membership proposition is sufficiently attractive, and relationship marketing sufficiently effective, to retain members and students.

Measuring the internal marketing plan

- Staff turnover and retention rates, absenteeism and dispute rates. These are general indicators of morale and esprit de corps, which might help to suggest whether staff are satisfied, secure and supported in their work. However, they are only indirect indicators, which may not correlate meaningfully to the internal marketing programme: other problems may be responsible for the figures.

- Post-training observation by coaches and mentors can be used to measure the success of the learning exercise and transfer of learning to the job.

- Feedback forms and attitude surveys (as well as informal feedback gathering and/or formal interviews by mentors and centre managers) may be used to gain feedback from participating staff: how effective they thought the briefing/coaching and communication was; what information needs were or were not met; what effect the new role emphasis has had on their job satisfaction; and so on.

- Critical incident analysis may be used to identify examples of best practice and success or problems and further training/support needs.

- Performance data will be gathered using the forms and systems provided: how many potential membership enquiries and new or upgraded memberships were signed up by each centre, and by each member of staff. This is a useful results-based measure of the success of internal marketing, according to the plan's objective, but it poses a motivational risk. It should be emphasised that results monitoring is for the purpose of support planning and award-giving: individual staff members will not be 'judged' or penalised for low sign-ups, and awards are celebratory, rather than purely competitive.

▶ **Assessment tip**

The real test of any marketing plan's effectiveness comes at implementation. Only by measuring marketing performance can corrective action can be taken when results are not as good as expected. You will need to demonstrate the quantitative and qualitative measures you can put in place to measure performance and the mechanism by which you can communicate results through the organisation. Marketing suffers from not always being effective at telling other parts of the organisation the contribution it is making.

The content of this Assignment brief will obviously vary according to the nature of the plan you are trying to measure; what marketing objectives you have set; and what kind of organisation you are focusing on. (For example, is it meaningful to talk about 'sales volume' or 'repeat sales'? Are media exposure, share of voice or market share a priority?) Even if you *know that* objectives-based evaluation is the most effective method, given your SMART objectives, note that you need to 'identify and evaluate a range of methods'... Note also that you could have included this section within your marketing plans for each stakeholder, under the 'monitoring and control' headings, if you wished.

This is more or less straight bookwork, as long as you ensure that all the methods you choose are relevant. We have just skimmed a range of possibilities, to show how broad your thinking needs to be – and how you need to tailor your methods to the circumstances.

Exemplar assignment brief: Task four

Critically analyse the leadership skills and approach required to make the marketing strategy and marketing plan a success. In so doing, critically assess your own leadership style and evaluate your personal development needs.

Recommend, with justification, how cultural change will be achieved and how the support of key stakeholders will be ensured.

> ▶ **Assessment tip**
>
> It is one thing to know and understand good marketing leadership practices, concepts and principles but another to implement them. Leaders might know what they should be doing but the organisation and environmental contexts present challenges to implementing improvements and change.

Clearly, BAM will have to undergo a process of change if it is to achieve its new strategy. This will require an enormous commitment from the senior management team to drive forward the changes required in the organisation. Even at the top of the organisation, there will be constraints and factors out of the control of the leader and influences and factors that have to be negotiated and navigated.

There is no one right leadership style, many factors influence what is possible (personal traits and skills), what is right (the situation and circumstances) and what is appropriate (ethical and social goals). Taking the best principles from the theory and reflecting on our changing social and business environment can help frame a leadership style that meets a variety of needs and allows for a range of adaptations as appropriate.

The leadership skills required to make the marketing strategy and marketing plan a success are the following:-

- **Self-confidence and energy**: a belief in the strategy and the motivation to ensure it understood by all levels of the organisation;

- **Persistence and determination:** a strong desire to ensure that the strategy is implemented so as to achieve its desired objectives;

- **Decisive, assertive and fair**: charisma, innovation and creativity;

- **Adaptable and co-operative:** a consultative approach will be required to ensure that people feel involved in the development of the strategy and have a stake in its success;

- **Humility:** the ability to accept and respect other people's views and opinions.

One area of increasing importance for a leader is emotional intelligence, This is described as 'the ability to monitor one's own and others' feelings, emotions, to discriminate among them and use this information to guide thinking and actions'. In particular, a leader needs to:

- **Identify emotions:** perceive emotions in himself/herself and others

- **Use emotions:** generate, use and feel emotion to communicate feelings, or employ them in thinking or creating, in order to maximise the potential of my team;

- **Manage emotions:** sometimes I can get stressed when under pressure. I need to develop the ability to control my emotions and in others to promote personal understanding and growth.

In so doing I believe I can be a more effective leader during this period of change in order to support the senior management team in inspiring, influencing developing others, and acting as a catalyst of change within the organisation. During this challenging period, I need to ensure that the organisation collaborates and communicates openly.

Leadership style at BAM

▶ **Assessment tip**

There are a wide variety of leadership models you could select here. Select one model that you can apply in depth to the issue under investigation in your assignment brief.

Generally, the leadership style that has been encouraged at BAM can best be described as 'Country Club Management' according to Blake and Mouton. On the whole, he organisation has attended to people's needs for satisfying relationships and has created a comfortable, friendly organisation, atmosphere and work tempo. This has created a cosy atmosphere that now is faced with global competition needs to change and to become more commercially edged.

In order to achieve its strategy it needs to become more concerned with achieving outcomes. This will require a change in leadership style amongst the senior and middle management team to drive forward the required change in direction.

A successful model to follow will be the Hersey and Blanchard based situational leadership model. This is based on 'readiness' (the followers ability and willingness to accomplish task) and the level of people the leader is attempting to influence. The leadership style reflects the amount of direction and support that the leader provides to their followers.

They describe leadership styles as four types of behaviour named S1 to S4:

- **S1 Telling:** Providing specific instructions and closely supervise performance. This is required where the readiness of the team to follow the course of action is low;

- **S2 Selling:** Explaining decisions, providing an opportunity for clarification. This is required where the team is willing but unable to follow the course of action because they do not have the necessary skills or competences;

- **S3 Participating:** Sharing ideas, to facilitate decision-making. This is required where the team is able to follow the course of action but unwilling;

- **S4 Delegating:** Devolving responsibility for decisions and implementation. This is required where the readiness of the team to follow the course of action is high.

The different styles require a different focus, either on the task or on the relationship between the leader and follower, depending on the situation. It is clear in discussing the strategy within the organisation that people are willing but feel at this stage unable to implement it confidently.

Therefore, in this situation, senior and middle management will have to take the lead, myself included and be more directive. My preferred style is to be participative but I understand that this style can only be effective once my team understand the new strategy and what it is expected and required to achieve.

I will also need to develop the ability to think creatively or differently and at any point in the development of the strategy. We also need to identify thought leaders within the organisation – celebrate and support those individuals who have a different point of view and are able to identify new solutions to new challenges. In the past, such people within the organisation have not stayed long enough in the organisation to make a real and lasting difference. We must now seek to retain and harness the insights such individuals can bring.

The BAM culture

The BAM culture, according to Charles Handy, can best be described as a power culture. This is typically only as strong as the central figure who exercises control through a small circle of executives who usually retain financial control. Politics are a feature of this culture and decisions are often based on political themes rather than for logical or operational reasons. Lack of formality means management development is difficult. Personal development is achieved through a system of apprenticeship to the central power and this special place is

The Chartered
Institute of Marketing

dependent on the quality of the relationship. People are promoted because of the people they know or get on well with, not because of what they do or have achieved.

In order to be effective in driving the strategy forward BAM needs to move towards a 'task culture'. This culture tends to encourage innovation and creativity and people are judged by results. Respect for people is based on their knowledge and expertise rather than status and position. There is high job satisfaction with an emphasis on group work. There is often no single individual in authority and power often lies in areas where the 'net' is stronger and points cross.

How change can be achieved

The challenge is to pull together the process of managing change with managing people through change. It is easy to focus on operations and tasks during change as there is a sense of urgency about getting things right. However, we can only get things right if we manage people.

A key phase in the management of change is to manage carefully the announcement of what will happen.. Employees should not become aware of plans for change via the grapevine, gossip and rumour.

We will need to ensure there is a timely announcement as part of a planned communication that reduces the potential for the shock of the new strategy. Senior management should present the requirement for change and invite employees to become involved in the process. It should emphasise the need for change and enable employees to express their concerns, hopes and fears.

This can be achieved through a number of mechanisms. Where possible the Chief Executive should meet with the organisation to deliver a keynote address outlining the new strategy, explain why it is needed and how it will be implemented. This would be effective in a series of workshops in which the senior management engaged with people to take them through the strategy in detail and to answer any questions. Full use should also be made of the BAM intranet to enable employees to participate in discussion forums and so on.

It is important during this stage that we understand the effect change will have on people and this will include uncertainty, a perception of a lack of control over personal performance and increasing frustration. Other areas of preoccupation are: a possible loss of responsibility, possible loss of social networks, lack of security, a sense of abandonment and feelings of incompetence as the realisation of newly defined roles emerge.

When change starts, employees embark on a journey that runs parallel to daily work routines. It is unsettling if this journey is not understood and people are not properly prepared or managed. It becomes threatening as the journey increasingly impacts on the daily work routines and the social climate. The personal journey involves phases people may go through during the change process. Different people will react in different ways. If change is managed properly, resistance will be minimal, and some of the more negative phases may be avoided. However, if change is not properly managed people may become stuck in the more unproductive modes of operation. Quiet resistance then becomes a way of life.

Another essential we must deal with is one of the less comfortable aspects of change, the necessity to make people redundant. Sometimes it is unavoidable and, as well as the distress for those who will be made redundant, it is upsetting and unsettling for those who remain. For those who have to be made redundant, some will deal with the experience better than others but all need support. If this is an outcome then we should helping people with CVs, practising interviews and helping them set up a network of contacts. This helps those who have to go but also signals to those who remain that managers care and will do what they can to help.

We should also establish 'change project teams'. We want to establish change teams that can minimise negative responses and behaviour and maximise positive. We cannot pretend it is going to be easy. However, the goal is to combine expertise and use the opportunity to design a team that will facilitate change.

We need to identify 'campaigners' – within the organisation, people who can see the benefits or gain in some way and are therefore enthusiastic about the change. They will be keen to help drive the change through. Establishing a climate of co-operation and recognising the value of all contributions can help alleviate explosive situations or withdrawal. Such individuals can help the management team pay more attention to the needs of people within the organisation and manage the change process.

In order to ensure that all stakeholders within the organisation feel valued, an extended period of consultation will need to take place to ensure that everyone is committed to the new strategic approach. Such an approach will help build rapport, even if the consultations have arisen due to conflict it is important to build rapport with all parties. Building respect and trust are vital if the strategy is to be widely accepted and adopted.

In terms of my own personal development, I will need to learn the following skills:

- **Question and listen** – Asking questions of my team will indicate that I am interested in their views, particularly if I learn to listen to the answers.

- **Exploring options** – learn to accept there are usually alternative solutions and these need to be discussed and evaluated for their suitability to both sides. Exploring options will help avoid being stuck in one place

We must allow time for employees to become familiar with new work routines and practices. There may still be some training, coaching or mentoring required. Employees will either be re-enforcing old social networks or building new ones. These networks should be encouraging behaviour that reflects the desired values of a marketing orientation. This is a time to embed new ways of doing things.

People will still be adapting to a different way of doing things and exploration of what works, what needs adjusting may still be required even when the strategy has been implemented. We must provide opportunities for review and learning from the process of change, the experiences and activities. This can be achieved through regular meetings with my team and informally through my dealings with colleagues across the organisation.

During change, it is easy to become wrapped up in the detail of internal activities and events. However, throughout the entire change project marketing is also responsible for making sure the focus on customers and other externals or stakeholders is not lost. During this period we need to be careful with our communications not to over promise during change. There can be a danger of communicating the vision long before it is achieved. There is nothing wrong with communicating the vision but keep in it perspective and ensure promises are honest and achievable, what can realistically be expected during periods of change. However, it will be vitally important to continually engage with our members and clients and ensure they are aware of the changes taking place and the benefits this will provide them.

5 How to avoid failing the assignment

From the Senior Examiner's report on the March 2012 assignment, it is possible to identify many key weaknesses:

- Theory or recommendations not being correctly applied, with associated loss of relevance or context. This can lead to discussions that could be generic, applying to any organisation

- The assignment should not be presented as a purely academic piece of work, as previously mentioned, you are expected to write in a professional way and in the required format. For the leadership part of the March 2012 paper, the examiner referred to the fact that many candidates used only bullet points, which meant that the discursive nature of the script was absent.

- It was noted that the weaker candidates ignored the aspects of competitiveness and sustainability as well as references to cultural and organisational change that is at the heart of this unit.

- Candidates would do well not to follow a strict formulaic approach, as it is noted that restricts creativity and individual thought.

- Poor presentation: the 'week in a drawer' is often cited as a good way to get a final and objective perspective on what you have done. Sometimes, on returning to the script, days later, candidates have been appalled at the naïve presentation of the arguments! A good 'acid test' is to think of yourself as a consultant. Would a CEO pay good money for your analysis and recommendations?

- A key differentiator among the papers, according to the examiner, was the differing levels of critical evaluation. Weaker candidates included a lot of description that needed to be developed, analysed and contextualised to the organisation.

- Only the stronger candidates reflected sufficiently on the implications of whether any change to strategy was incorporated, or not.

- From the Senior Examiner's Report on the June, 2012 assessment, we find the following as reasons for not achieving a pass grade: lack of ability to address all aspects of the task; lack of application (eg, providing a framework, or model, but then not applying it); poor structure (eg, discussion of the Marketing Mix coming before marketing objectives); failure to discuss the implications of the resources in developing the actual strategy; poor knowledge of strategy formulation/development, linked to poor use of the audit; very little critical analysis; lack of a coherent marketing strategy; failure to identify the key drivers and pressures on the organisation.

CHAPTER 4

Managing corporate reputation

Topic list

1 Unit overview and syllabus

1.1 Unit overview

Generally, the principal task of the assessment – worth 60% of the mark- will evaluate how well you can respond to challenging corporate reputational issues, strategically, using insight. Can you demonstrate an aptitude to respond rapidly, using the right methods, approaches and frameworks?. The main themes of the unit are: the reputation of organisations, the advantages, in corporate terms, of carefully building a strong positive reputation in the marketplace and the huge danger when that reputation is in any way tarnished.

In a moment, we will look at cases where this latter has happened.

You may be asked to prepare a White Paper, or perhaps, a Discussion Paper. In the Appendix, you can find a description and suggested heading for work like this (see Formats).

For the first task of the assessment, you will be required to show strategic insight and the capacity to deal with issues of corporate reputation in your own organisation, or one of your choice, which you know well. Typically, you are asked to write a report showing that you understand fully the theories, principles and practices of developing organisational reputation, particularly focusing on the main elements of trustworthiness, responsibility and credibility.

In this report, the examiner will be expecting that you will apply effectively some of the major concepts deconstructed from reputation itself, using these as a means to evaluate the organisation's performance, providing key recommendations as to possible improvements. Obviously, such recommendations must take into account the consequences for the organisation.

For the second part (40% of the mark), you may chose one of three tasks and these may take the form of a white paper, a report, an article or some other format. Any aspect of the syllabus, which we present next, could be the subject of your work (see also 'Formats', in the Appendix).

The pattern of each task of the assignment will always be:

- **Theory**, (explaining what you know about the theme, in conceptual terms
- **Evaluation and Application**, (a critical analysis of the situation, the theory and how it can be applied, with what results)
- **Recommendations**, (carefully crafted suggestions, supported by theory and factual evidence of ways to improve performance in reputational terms).

As mentioned earlier in this workbook, the examiner will be expecting that you approach these tasks in a professional as well as academic manner. Please refer to previous comments regarding 'postgraduateness'.

Finally, this unit offers optional elements and it is important to focus on **why** you would take a particular option, linking it to your areas of interest, or your company's. Examiners say that one massive failing of students, in this area, is to duplicate Question 1, or aspects of it. It is the ability to respond to the optional elements in their own right that examiners are looking for.

▶ **Assessment tip**

There is great variety in the way that certain terminology is used in this area of marketing communications.

For example:

'Corporate Reputation is the set of meanings by which an organisation is known and through which stakeholders describe, remember and relate to it. .....' Adapted from Dowling (1996)

'Corporate Reputation is the overall estimation in which an organisation is held by its constituents....' Adapted from Fombrun (1996)

'Corporate Reputation is an individual's collective representation of past images of an organisation..... established over time' Cornelissen (2007)

On reading widely, therefore, it's easy to become confused as to the exact meaning of the key terms Corporate Identity, Corporate Image and Corporate Reputation.

In the *Managing Corporate Reputation* Study Text, you'll find precise definitions of these terms.

1.1.1 Why is Corporate Reputation important?

It is important because of:

Input factors: reputation allows the firm to obtain the best value in terms of suppliers and therefore services and materials and also in human resources and the pool of knowledge.

Output factors: an organisation's ability to secure shareholder value, market share, bank loans and so forth. In a word, the confidence that is shown in its activities.

According to Fombrun (1996), an organisation's reputation is composed of:

- Credibility
- Trustworthiness
- Reliability
- Responsibility

The First Connect debacle

Managing the reputation of your organisation is an important, serious matter. No amount of advertising can convince public opinion of your credibility once trust is lost.

Stakeholders and investors, in particular, are scrutinising corporate image and any signs of damage are quickly reflected in the price of stock.

So it was in October 2012, with the First Connect Group. After celebrating their victory over Virgin Trains for the franchise of the West Coast mainline, share prices plummeted when the Government announced irregularities in the bidding process.

First Group now (November 2012) see their image tarnished, not just because of those miscalculations, in which they have no fault, but because of the allegations that First Connect was grossly overbidding for the franchise.

In the words of Sir Richard Branson: 'the bid was insane' and this is the residual image.

In some quarters, it was thought that First Connect rather rashly wanted their hands on the franchise but had made contingency plans for an eventual, likely failure. It would seem that First Connect overplayed their hand, causing Branson to demand a Judicial Review, the threat of which brought the errors to light.

In desperation, the Government asked Virgin to carry on temporarily – probably a bit more than temporarily – while First Connect comes out of the blunder with their reputation seriously affected.

1.1.2 The Reputational Value lifecycle

According to van Riel & Fombrun (2007):

Revenues, profits, with a market assessment of future prospects – with a central focus of Corporate Reputation – leads to enhanced shareholder values, which leads to investment in corporate initiatives, citizenship and communications, which leads to supportive stakeholders and endorsement of what we do.

Northern Rock taken over by Virgin Group

Although Northern Rock enjoyed considerable popularity in the North East of the United Kingdom - where it sponsored the Newcastle United football club, the Newcastle Falcons Rugby Club (whose grounds it purchased for £15 million, some weeks before its bail-out) as well as providing the Northern Rock Charitable foundation – in the rest of the country and for the world at large, the brand is synonymous with the debacle of what came to be known as the 'credit crunch'.

Northern Rock was best known for the alarming image of panicked customers making a 'run on the bank', the first since the 18th Century, after it had to ask a loan facility from the Bank of England, to replace money market funding during the credit crisis in 2007. As no commercial buyer was forthcoming, the Labour Government of the day took it into public ownership in 2008.

In January 2012, under the new Coalition Government, the bank was finally sold to the Virgin Group for around half of the value of the tax-payers' bail-out.

Here, we see huge problems of corporate identity and image facing the buyer, whose public *persona* is, of course, Sir Richard Branson. Branson is known for his flamboyant lifestyle, as an adventurer and a free-wheeling entrepreneur, with interests in all kinds of businesses from Spaceships to Trains and Gymnasiums to Holidays.

The enormous diversity of Virgin Group investments has what could be perceived as a downside, as reflected in its dissipated Corporate Identity and Image. A page showing all the Virgin Group logos is a riotous confusion of colour and graphics.

How would you set about re-branding disgraced Northern Rock as Virgin Money? See the end of this chapter.

1.2 Unit characteristics

The strength and magnitude of the reputation of an organisation, entity or destination represents the way in which a complex range of stakeholders perceive it. All too often, a gap develops between the way an organisation intends to be seen and the reality. This can be due to a range of forces, some slow, foreseeable and manageable and some sudden, unforeseen and relatively unmanageable.

All can result in organisational underperformance, destabilisation, financial difficulties, leadership change, a fall in market valuation, and even difficulty in raising finance or recruiting the right personnel.

This unit explores ways in which organisations can minimise the gap and avoid these potentially serious issues.

1.2.1 Overarching learning outcomes

By the end of this unit, students should be able to:

- Critically evaluate the way organisations develop their identities and some organisations use these to form images and assign reputational status.

- Critically analyse the elements that contribute to the identity that an organisation projects to its stakeholders, sometimes through a corporate brand.

- Critically evaluate linkage between how an organisation wants to be seen and how **it is** seen, namely by corporate communications.

Students will normally base their learning and development of these issues on an organisation. However, some may choose to use this unit to explore the reputational development of a place. This might involve for example, a tourist destination (eg, country or region), a business area (eg seaport or park) or a city or town.

The detail specified in this syllabus is based on ideas, practice and the research literature relating to corporate branding, communications and reputation.

▶ **Assessment tip**

For the purposes of this module and your assignment – and unless otherwise instructed in the assignment brief – you should not use the term *organisational identity*. The basis on which this syllabus was created was that Corporate Identity refers to the identity the organisation wishes to convey about itself to internal and external stakeholders: **the desired identity.**

As a general comment, Corporate Identity is the marketer's perspective, whereas organisational identity is the HR perspective.

1.3 The Syllabus

Part 1 – Understanding the nature and characteristics of reputational management (weighting 25%)

SECTION 1 – Developing the rationale for managing corporate reputation

1.1.1	Critically evaluate the context and concepts relating to corporate reputation: ■ Development, evolution and perception ■ Corporate image versus corporate identity ■ Context: industrial, not-for-profit, competitive, societal, political ■ Criteria: credibility, trustworthiness, reliability and responsiveness
1.1.2	Justify the importance and significance of managing an organisation's corporate reputation: ■ Financial performance ■ Managing shareholder value ■ Improved competitiveness ■ Relative ease of recruitment
1.1.3	Identify the forces that can influence an organisation's reputation, and develop forecasts concerning their level of current and potential influence: ■ External forces: environmental, financial, political, social, industry-wide, legal, technological, community-based ■ Relational: competitive and collaborative strategies, resources, mergers/acquisitions, repositioning ■ Internal forces: resources, political, strategy, structure, behaviour, communication climate

SECTION 2 – Determining the scope of corporate reputation

1.2.1	Critically assess the compatibility of an organisation's corporate strategy, structure, systems and culture with its positioning and reputation: ■ Vision, mission, values, objectives ■ Organisational structure and culture ■ Organisational communication climate ■ Perception and positioning
1.2.2	Develop processes leading to the identification of key external and internal stakeholders, and understand the nature of associated communication programmes: ■ Investors – investor relations ■ Customers – marketing communications ■ Employees – internal communications ■ Government – public affairs ■ The public – public relations
1.2.3	Propose and justify the use of a portfolio of broad indicators to evaluate the strength of an organisation's reputation: ■ ROI ■ Brand equity ■ Shareholder value ■ Media comment

Part 2 – Managing the dimensions of an organisation's reputation (weighting 25%)

SECTION 1 – Understanding the current corporate reputation

2.1.1	Critically evaluate the corporate 'character' (personality) of an organisation
	▪ Organisation culture
	▪ Strategy; mission, values and positioning, formulation process
	▪ Organisational structure
	▪ Communication climate
2.1.2	Critically assess the strength and potential of the corporate identity and/or brand
	▪ Meaning: visual, organisational, corporate, visual identity versus strategic identity
	▪ Identity mix: behaviour, communication and symbolism
	▪ Brand strategy: structure, architecture and promise
	▪ Systems and processes, eg formalistic or organic, developing or established, communication culture
	▪ Measurement of reputation using commercial systems, eg Brand Asset Valuator, BrandZ, Equitrend, Brand Power, USA's Most Admired, Reputation Quotient, RepTrack

SECTION 2 – Developing corporate brands

2.2.1	Critically evaluate the nature of corporate brands and make recommendations concerning any gap between identity and image:
	▪ Definitions
	▪ Elements: differentiation, transferability, psychic value, recall, premium
	▪ Typologies: Olins, Kammerer, van Riel
	▪ Drivers: strategy, organisational, employee, value
	▪ Levels of corporate endorsement
	▪ Re-branding
2.2.2	Propose changes to enhance the systems, structure and processes necessary to support the management of corporate reputation:
	▪ Communication audits
	▪ Targeting stakeholder groups
	▪ Targeting employees
	▪ Reputation platforms
	▪ Corporate stories and story telling
	▪ Corporate positioning

Part 3 – Developing effective corporate communications (weighting 50%)

SECTION 1 – Determining the dimensions of corporate communications

3.1.1	Critically appraise the nature and characteristics of corporate communications: ■ Definition ■ Corporate communications mix: management, organisational, marketing ■ Principal activities: internal, investor, marketing, public affairs, issues management
3.1.2	Critically assess the different reasons for using corporate communication: ■ Aims and purpose: four visions ■ Tasks, eg informing, exploring, relating, negotiating and mixed formats ■ Circumstances, eg periodic reporting, crisis, merger/acquisition, repositioning, strategic change, decline ■ Stimulating change, eg knowledge, attitudes, behaviour
3.2.1	Critically evaluate the different methods through which corporate communications can be delivered in order to deliver effective messages and enhance reputation: ■ Tools: corporate advertising, public relations, sponsorships ■ Media: offline and digital/online ■ Symbolism: logos, names, signage, music, styling, uniforms, design and architecture ■ Behaviour: employees, management performance, corporate, brand, communications
3.2.2	Formulate approaches to corporate communications that are investor-focused and contextually determined: ■ Roles of investor relations, eg compliance, relationships, building (reputation) ■ Purpose: create demand for shares, reduce churn, present past performance, predict future performance, manage perceptions
3.2.3	Formulate approaches to corporate communications that are customer-focused and contextually determined: ■ Tools: advertising, sales promotion, personal selling, marketing, public relations ■ Media: offline/online ■ Messages: informational and emotional dimensions of engagement ■ Experience marketing
3.2.4	Formulate approaches to corporate communications that are employee-focused and contextually determined: ■ Types: structure, flow, content and climate ■ Roles: efficiency, shared meaning, connectivity, satisfaction ■ Intellectual and emotional engagement ■ Messages: information and emotional dimensions of engagement within the organisation
3.2.5	Formulate approaches to corporate communications that are government-focused and contextually determined: ■ Breadth: regulators, legislators, elected officials and appointed representatives ■ Public affairs ■ Lobbying, relationships, timing and objectivity
3.2.6	Formulate approaches designed to defend an organisation's reputation: ■ Nature of issues management: detection, marshalling and strategy ■ Crisis communications: nature, risk analysis, agenda setting, response and rumour management

How North Face betrayed its customer base

North Face, the Californian supplier of outdoor apparel and equipment has been something of an iconic brand.

In the UK, so many BBC TV presenters were filmed wearing their down-filled North Face coats, with its prominent logo, that some took exception to it, claiming that the BBC was guilty of product placement! Then in February, 2012, the storm broke over the heads of those responsible for the brand.

North Face, a brand established forty years ago, promotes itself as a strongly ethical company with an honest approach to sourcing and manufacturing and global positioning that encompasses sustainability and eco-friendliness as a given. Its website goes to the point of proclaiming an extensive 'Sustainability Programme', with what appears to be a searching self-examination of its progress towards Corporate Social Responsibility.

Under the headline 'Community', the customer can find the following:

'Being a responsible business means serving the larger community and enriching people's lives in a way that draws upon our company's passions and capabilities. Our sense of community extends far beyond the walls of our offices to encompass our associates, suppliers, consumers, our industry, our communities and organizations that share our interests'.

In such a case, we can imagine the stress for North Face executives to see their brand plastered all over headlines from The Daily Mail to The Telegraph, with claims that the feathers (down) used in the jackets was being sourced from Hungarian poultry farms, specifically from the grey geese that are reared for Foie Gras. Previously, North Face had denied any connection with foie gras.

Now it so happens that foie gras, very much appreciated in France and many other countries has a particularly unpleasant production process, inasmuch that it comes from the diseased livers of the said geese. The disease is deliberately caused by the practice of force-feeding of the geese with metal tubes down the throat, to the point that the liver becomes swollen, obviously causing much distress to the poor animal. Uproar!

Previously, the depth of negative feeling towards foie gras, both in America and in the UK, was exemplified by the incident of celebrity butcher Jack O' Shea being forcibly removed by Security from Harrods after selling foie gras 'under the counter' with the codename French Fillet.

Can you imagine your company, famous for its responsible approach to the sourcing of materials, under the ensuing attack. How would you react? What effect might this stain on the reputation of the company have on sales? What should executives do? (At the end of this chapter we provide some clues)

2 The assignment brief

You will be assessed by assignment for this unit. This unit lends itself to the assignment route for assessment because it is more realistic to be able to spend time reflecting on corporate reputation issues in detail. Students tend to find assignments very useful as a learning tool especially when they are related to their own organisations.

For your assignment you are encouraged to use your own organisation to base your answers on. Of course, if you are not currently working then you can:

(a)   Find a host company who would be willing to let you use them as a project (often charities and small local organisations are interested in any offer of free 'consultancy' work carried out as part of student projects.

(b)   Consider whether a previous company you have worked with would be suitable.

(c)   Discuss with your tutor the use of a case study company.

▸ **Assessment tip**

Remember you are being assessed on your ability to prepare a high quality assignment and not whether you are working for a suitable type of organisation (although by this stage in your studies it is likely that you will be). Often the most interesting assignments are written for the most unusual organisations so do not feel that because you may not work for a 'cutting edge' market-orientated company you are disadvantaged in any way.

2.1 Format of the assignment

You assignment will have to complete two tasks, one core and one elective.

- **Task one** – is a compulsory core task and worth 60% of the marks.

- **Task two** – is an elective and you have to choose one task from three possible options. This task is worth 40% of the marks.

2.2 The specimen assignment

Task one: Report (60% weighting)

Justifying the management of corporate reputation

You have been requested by your CEO to prepare a report in which you investigate the quality of the organisation's current reputation. In particular, you should:

- Critically assess the current strength of the organisation's reputation

- Prepare a case arguing for the formal establishment or development of a corporate reputation management process

- Recommend and justify processes, structures and systems necessary to improve corporate reputation.

The aim of this report is to determine the organisation's reputation, to consider the forces that shape it, to consider the benefits that arise from a strong reputation and to suggest ways in which the organisation should actively manage its reputation. Reference to the political and financial consequences of implementing the recommendations is expected.

Note: This is an individual assignment; as such the report must be completed individually and not as part of a group.

Word count: 4,000 words, excluding relevant appendices

1.1.1; 1.1.2; 1.1.3; 1.2.1; 1.2.3; 3.2.1; 3.2.6

Table 4.1   Mark scheme – Task one

Marking criteria	Marks available
Critical assessment of the current strength of the organisation's reputation	30
Preparation of a case arguing for the formal establishment or development of a corporate reputation management process	30
Justified recommendations for processes, structures and systems necessary to improve corporate reputation	30
Format and Presentation ■ Relevance to the tasks ■ Use concepts and frameworks to support arguments, points and recommendations ■ Professional tone and required format ■ Appropriate use of examples to illustrate points ■ Appropriate referencing (Harvard APA).	10
Total	100

Task two: Elective section (40% weighting)

This is your elective section, there are three options and you must choose one to complete.

Task two option 1: Report, Brand drivers

The aim of this task is to evaluate the strength of the drivers of an organisation's corporate brand and to make recommendations to change or improve support for the brand.

Using an organisation with which you are familiar, you are to write a report for consideration by the CEO and the Board of Directors. The report should evaluate the strength of internal support, and in particular the four drivers that underpin your organisation's corporate brand.

You are to make recommendations to improve support for the brand and in particular you should:

■ Examine the concept of corporate branding and the drivers thought to underpin it

■ Evaluate the relative strength of each of the four main corporate brand drivers within your chosen organisation

■ Recommend ways in which your organisation could improve internal support for its corporate brand.

Whilst your report should focus on the drivers, you may examine other aspects of your organisation that you feel are relevant to the delivery and relative effectiveness of the corporate brand. Reference to the political and financial consequences of the recommendations is expected.

Note: This is an individual assignment; as such the report must be completed individually and not as part of a group.

Word count: 2,000 words, excluding relevant appendices

2.1.1; 2.1.2; 3.1.1; 3.1.2; 3.1.3; 3.2.1

Table 4.2   Mark scheme – Report: Brand drivers

Marking criteria	Marks available
Examination of the concept of corporate branding and the drivers that underpin it	30
Evaluation of the relative strength of each of the four main corporate brand drivers within the organisation	30
Recommendation of ways in which the organisation could improve internal support for its corporate brand.	30
Format and Presentation • Relevance to the tasks • Use concepts and frameworks to support arguments, points and recommendations • Professional tone and required format • Appropriate use of examples to illustrate points • Appropriate referencing (Harvard APA).	10
Total	100

Task two option two: Article, Corporate symbolism

This task requires candidates to write an article for submission and subsequent publication in a professional or practitioner magazine or journal. The article concerns a critical review of your organisation's use of symbolism to communicate with a range of stakeholders.

In particular, you should evaluate the organisation's name, logo, strapline, use of colour, fonts, work-wear and uniforms, architecture, letterheads and other visual artefacts and instruments used to communicate with stakeholders.

The article should reflect on the development of recent changes in the visual identity, and make recommendations concerning any relationship between visual identity and the organisation's corporate strategy and positioning.

Note: This is an individual assignment; as such the report must be completed individually and not as part of a group.

Word count: 2,000 words, excluding relevant appendices

Syllabus references

1.2.1; 1.2.2; 2.1.1; 2.1.2; 3.1.3

Table 4.3   Mark scheme – Article, Corporate symbolism

Marking criteria	Marks available
Evaluation of the organisation's name, logo, strapline, use of colour, fonts, workwear and uniforms, architecture, letterheads and other visual artefacts and instruments used to communicate with stakeholders	30
Analysis of the development or recent changes in visual identity	30
Recommendations concerning the relationship between visual identity and the organisation's corporate strategy and positioning.	30
Format and Presentation • Relevance to the tasks • Use concepts and frameworks to • Support arguments, points and recommendations • Professional tone and required format • Appropriate use of examples to illustrate points • Appropriate referencing (Harvard).	10
Total	100

Task two option three: Paper, Internal communications

One of the key problems faced by many organisations concerns the quality and extent to which internal communications can be used to engage employees.

Following some success using the Internet to communicate with employees, it has been agreed with your manager that you are to write a paper about the use of technology in internal communications. It is intended that the paper will be part of a drive to improve the organisation's reputation. This will be achieved by using internal communications to enable employees to identify more closely with the organisation's values.

Your paper should be based on the effective use of a range of digital technologies, not just the Internet, in order to improve internal communications. Consideration should be given to:

- An assessment of the organisation's overall communication climate and the extent to which the internal communications fit with the corporate brand strategy

- A demonstration of the key ways in which digital technology should be used to engage employees

- Recommendation of a process or series of actions that can enhance the quality of internal communications.

The aim of this paper is to evaluate the form and nature of the internal communications, to identify problems and to make practical recommendations to improve them through the use of digital technology. Reference to any financial and political consequences of the recommendations is expected.

Note: This is an individual assignment; as such the report must be completed individually and not as part of a group.

Word count: 2,000 words, excluding relevant appendices

Syllabus References

2.2.2; 3.1.2; 3.2.1; 3.2.4

Assessment Tip

On choosing an organisation that is not your current place of work, you will need to do considerable research in order to understand the challenges and the reasons behind them. Some companies publish a great deal of information in the form of company reports, newsletters, blogs, house magazines and the like, however this will be the "public" face of the organisation. For an 'insider' view, you will need to have unusual access to information, which can only really be obtained from employees (or perhaps through the PR companies with which they work).

Table 4.4   Mark scheme – Paper, Internal communications

Marking criteria	Marks available
Assessment of the organisation's overall communication climate and the extent to which the internal communications fit with the corporate brand strategy	30
Demonstration of the key ways in which digital technology should be used to engage employees	30
Recommendations of a process or series of actions that can enhance the quality of internal communications.	10
Format and Presentation ■ Relevance to the tasks ■ Use concepts and frameworks to support arguments, points and recommendations ■ Professional tone and required format ■ Appropriate use of examples to illustrate points ■ Appropriate referencing (Harvard APA).	10
Total	**100**

Appendix

Provide a brief background to your organization, its customer base, position in the market, and product/service range (up to a maximum of two sides of A4, no marks awarded).

Syllabus references

1.2, 1.3, 1.4, 1.6, 2.1, 2.3, 2.4, 2.5, 2.6, 2.7, 3.2, 3.3, 3.4, 3.5, 3.6, 3.7, 3.8, 4.2, 4.3

- Maximum word count for rationale: 500 words

- Maximum word count for the Marketing plan: 2,500 words (excluding relevant appendices)

- Maximum word count for the report: 3,000 words (excluding relevant appendices)

▸ **Assessment tip**

We have shown the Assessment and Marking criteria within one table so that you can see how the two are similar. In the assignment, you will be given these separately, so look to see where marks are awarded for each assessment criteria.

---

3 How to prepare for your assignment

3.1 Before you receive your assignment

There are a number of preparatory tasks that you can complete before you are given your assignment.

(a) Read the study text and complete the activities

(b) Compile a company background (even if you are not directly asked for one it will be useful to include one in the appendix for your examiner).

(c) Think about real instances of brand reputation management, events and crises which may have occurred etc within your own organisation. How might these have been improved? What would you do differently?

(d) Start to gather materials to consider how your organisation manages its reputation planning. This is likely to take a significant amount of time to complete. It is also worth discussing your organisations reputation with a range of internal and external stakeholders with whom you can contact either formally or informally. Begin this process as early into your studies as possible and treat it as a mini research project.

(e) Familiarise yourself with the CIM guidelines for the unit.

We will assume that you are completing your reading as you study. You can find out about writing your company background in section 1 of the workbook.

We will now look at the key aspects of the CIM guidelines.

3.2 CIM guidance

The following notes pick out the key points that you **MUST** adhere to from the CIM's instruction for candidates. It also gives you tips about how to succeed by using these notes to your advantage.

3.2.1 Context

- The assignment should be **based on your own organisation** or an organisation you are familiar with. You should discuss the organisation you plan to use with your tutor.

- Write a brief **overview of the organisation** chosen, including legal classification, product or service offered, target market and structure. This should be included in the **appendix** (please see section 1 of this workbook for further information about writing your company background). No marks will be allocated to the background and it will not count against word count limits.

- Do not include **sensitive data** from the chosen organisation or create an anonymous name for the organisation so that it cannot be identified from your work.

- Each assignment must be completed **individually**, not as part of a group.

3.2.2 Working with your tutor

- You are entitled **individual tutorial** time for this unit.

- You are able to discuss with your tutor your **choice of organisation and any questions** about the assignment.

- You are allowed to gain **feedback on one written assignment draft**. Do not ask your tutor to look at your improved draft because they are not permitted by the CIM to coach you or provide any more feedback.

- Your tutor will **not** be able to tell you the grade a piece of work is likely to achieve.

3.2.3 Word count

Word counts always cause students concern. At the beginning it seems like a daunting task to be able to actually write the required number of words. Amazingly, by the time you have completed your first draft the problem is very likely to have transformed into a major word reduction exercise. Writing succinctly and clearly is far more difficult to achieve than endless pages of 'waffle'.

- You must remain within **+10%** of the specified word count. This means that if you have a word count of 1000 words you must not write more than 1100 words. In this unit you may be given a **page limit**, in which case you should stick to the number of pages requested.

- You must **state** the number of words on the **front page** of your assignment.

- Headings, index, references, bibliographies, appendices and tables **do not count towards** your word limit. Within this module however it has been specified that you have a the following limits to adhere to:

   (i)   Core task – 4000 words
   (ii)   Elective task – 2000 words

- **Diagrams and tables** are encouraged however if **all or most** of your work is presented in this format then they **will be counted** towards your word limit. With a marketing audit and a marketing plan, it is expected that you include tables and other similar formats within the appendix (as outlined above).

3.2.4 Appropriate appendix items

Typically students try to put lots of excess information into an appendix as a means to overcome the word count limit. To do this is a dangerous strategy because often key information is overlooked by the examiner and the overall flow of the proposal is jeopardised. The golden rules for appendices are:

- Number the appendix and only include things that you have/will refer to in the main report. Nobody will read an item in an appendix if you have not explicitly directed them to it.

- Essential information that you require your audience to read because it is key to the point you are trying to make should be in the main report.

- Don't use the appendix as a means to prove that you have gathered lots of information- you are expected to do this anyway. You will not gain favour with an examiner for your lack of ability to synthesise the information if you put too much into an appendix.

The Chartered
Institute of Marketing

3.2.5 Plagiarism

Copying someone else's work or quoting from another source without referencing the source will be regarded as plagiarism. To avoid being suspected of plagiarism, ensure that you Harvard reference all sources as described in section 1 of this workbook.

Candidates found guilty of plagiarism may be:

- Disqualified from CIM membership
- Refused award of the unit or qualification
- Refused the right to retake the unit.

Remember to submit electronic copies of your work in the procedure specified by your tutor so that it may be passed through anti-plagiarism software by the CIM.

3.2.6 Assessment criteria, Mark schemes and Grade descriptors

Assessment criteria and marking scheme

The assessment criteria are useful because they outline what the examiner is looking for when assessing you. It is linked to the marking scheme which you will also be privy to. You should pay careful attention to these because they will give you a good indication of the level of content that is required in each section of your work.

▶ **Assessment tip**

It is highly advisable to use the assessment criteria as a basis for the structure of your submission piece that you are asked to complete as tasks.

As soon as you receive your assignment, it would be a good idea to establish which assessment or marking criteria relates to each individual task. Sometimes the Institute may outline the criteria next to the task, but not always and so you should be prepared to go through these and categorise where you are able to obtain marks.

Grade descriptors

Grade descriptors are also available on the CIM website and in the Appendix to this book. You should look through these because they outline what candidates need to demonstrate in order to achieve the various grades. Sometimes the grade descriptors are also appended to the assignment brief.

---

4 Tackling the assignment

4.1 The assignment, step by step

You will be very familiar with tackling assignments by now. The formats given in the sample you have experienced before:

For example:

- **Report** (covered in Marketing Leadership and Planning)
- **Article** (covered in Emerging Themes)

With any of these, the process for tackling the assignment will remain consistent.

You should be well practiced at tacking assignments using the process outlined below. Although there are differences in the length, the process will be equally valid for the core and elective tasks.

Step 1	'Unpack' the question. Also ensure you pay particular attention to the guidance section within the assignment. This will be particularly detailed for Task 1.
Step 2	Research relevant theories – begin with the Study Text, then CIM core reading, look for relevant research papers in this area and industry information and reports.
Step 3	Conduct internal research on 'how things operate' within your own organisation.
Step 4	Go through your 'write and review' process as described in Section 1 of this workbook.

4.2 How to pass the assignment

Adapted from a report by the Senior Examiner

The dominant themes running through all of the tasks are strategy, reputation and corporate communication. Surprisingly, these themes have not been fully understood by all candidates, nor has the need to make responses at the postgraduate level (as mentioned previously).

Candidates can download a paper from the CIM website that explains what this implies (we also cover 'postgraduateness' in Chapter 1 of this book).

Examiners are looking for:

- Identification of the appropriate models, concepts and theories.

- Demonstration of exceptional understanding of the issues.

- Application of the theories and concepts in practice.

- A senior management approach to the solution of problems.

- Evidence of reliable, valid and incisive range of recommendations.

- Complex approaches to problem solving in unpredictable situations.

- The provision of engaging, innovative and effective response, supported by business-related approaches.

- All elements of the task to be tackled, demonstrating real value.

- A strategic approach to the final recommendations and to the task overall.

A key piece of guidance from CIM is the provision of command words such as 'critically evaluate' as well as 'appraise', 'analyse', 'review' and 'make recommendations'. Such words are there to provide a guide for what is expected.

All candidates must demonstrate an ability to apply knowledge and critically assess it within an organisational context.

Those candidates who are critical, evaluative and apply their answers as required by each task will score more highly than those who merely describe or explain, without elaborating their answers, or providing depth

In essence, the examining team are asking: 'would we, as employers, actually select the candidate to do the job of managing and developing an organisation's corporate reputation? Can the candidate follow a brief, address the task in hand and deliver a value-added piece of work?'

The assessment team are looking for candidates to be creative, innovative and business-savvy in their approach, showing business acumen, aligned with the corporate reputation issues, proposing strategic-level recommendations that would enhance organisational corporate reputation

In the words of the Senior Examiner, in the March 2012 Report:

 The Chartered Institute of Marketing

'Those candidates who were critical, evaluative and applied their answers as required by each task, scored more highly than those who merely described or explained without elaborating their answers, or providing depth. Candidates with 'A' grade papers were few but a pleasure to read and had evidently read widely around the topic area and drew on a wide range of references including a range of text books and journal articles, as well as trade press and examples from trade and industry. As a result, they had extensive contributions to make, due to their wider reading and then applied relevant frameworks in a strategic way to the organisation, addressing more widely the tasks at hand'.

Also from the Report, we can find the following recommendations regarding **Presentation**.

Candidates should:

- Correctly structure their response and follow the structure of the task.
- Read the guidelines carefully and include all sections required.
- 'Signpost' sections to guide the reader through their response.
- Ensure the use of clear headings, sub-headings, bold headings and numbered points and sections.
- Include introductions and conclusions.
- Use the same size font and font type, not a variety.
- Ensure all diagrams have titles, sources and justification for inclusion.
- Avoid the overuse of lists (listing points, but not explaining them).
- Write to the wordcount.
- Proofread the work before submission.
- Ensure all references are included in the reference list and according with the Harvard system.

4.3 Preferred answer structure in a typical case

The Senior Examiner has thoughtfully provided us with the following (after all, the examiners want you to pass). In consideration of the CSR part of the assignment, the preferred answer structure could be:

- Introduction, in order to establish the context and plan of the answer.
- A clear understanding of what CSR is and an examination of theory, concepts and ideas relating to CSR and its relevance to building corporate reputation.
- An appraisal of the rationale, strategies and methods that the organisation uses to communicate its activities relating to corporate social responsibility.
- A critical evaluation of the quality, approach, transparency and accessibility of the organisation's current communications relating to CSR.
- A set of strategic recommendations that explore how the organisation could improve the way it communicates its CSR-related activities.
- A brief consideration of the political and financial implications of these recommendations.
- A short conclusion (not a summary).
- A reference list.

▶ **Assessment tip**

The examiners will appreciate a comprehensive list of references and can see it as evidence of careful research. You should include a wide variety of sources, including journal articles, which may be listed separately from book sources. Blogs and other online sources are also acceptable, but must be carefully referenced, using the Harvard system.

4.4 How to fail the assessment!

The Senior Examiner has referred to typical problems that result in 'D', 'E' and 'F' grades. These candidates:

- Failed to convince the examiners that they understood the topics

- Did not demonstrate extensive reading, which is a prerequisite of this unit. This is also reflected in poor referencing

- Did not implement or apply concepts , as instructed

- Did not follow assignment guidelines (a common fault)

- Wrote assignments that lacked suitable concepts, were merely descriptive and showed limited reading

- In terms of the recommendations, formulaic responses were sometimes put forward, as well as too much focus on short-term tactical considerations. The political and financial consequences were often ignored

- The marking scheme of the 'Magic Formula' (Presentation 10%; Concept 15%; Application 30% and Evaluation 45%) is used as a broad directional instrument by examiners rather than a precise tool for tightly marking the answers. Some candidates are struggling to understand the balance of how these marks are applied. It seems that the main focus is on concept and less on application and evaluation

According to the Senior Examiner, the elective tasks rarely attracted more than a bare pass. In some cases there was even duplicate material from the core task.

'Many of those in the lower grades did not appear to understand strategy, could not write critically, presented basic or naïve answers, could not reference correctly and were not writing at the postgraduate level' (from the Senior Examiner's Report).

The Chartered Institute of Marketing

5 Extracts from a 'good' assessment

From the Senior Examiner's Report June 2012, we can find the following sample assessment, which is revealing of examiners' thinking in terms of what constitutes a good response.

The requirement was : 'to critically appraise the current use of communications with the public OR the government in your selected organisation'.

An excerpt from what was considered a good paper follows. The organisation name has been changed to XXX.

Two years ago XXX was offered an exhibition stand at the Labour Party Conference in Manchester. We were dipping our toe in the world of 'public affairs'. This autumn, no longer the novice, we will be bringing informed debate to all three conferences.

What is public affairs and why is it crucial for HE institutions?

As XXX grows more comfortable with public affairs, public affairs is constantly shifting and evolving. This is to be expected as it reacts and adapts to changes in government, business and society. Many interpret public affairs as government relations but it is much wider than this as Senator George Mitchell describes: 'It is more than just lobbying politicians. At its heart is the ability to understand politics, decision-making, government infra-structure and policymaking'.

Lobbying: the actions of individuals, groups and organisations to access and influence, is arguably the most recognisable part of public affairs. This, in itself, can be a problem. It has always been viewed with some suspicion and 'lobbying' has become a much-maligned term. The recent and extensive media coverage of the Leveson Enquiry into the culture, practice and ethics of the press, has thrown the spotlight firmly on issues of political access and influence.

A House of Commons Select committee looked into the influence of lobbying on Whitehall in 2008 because 'whilst lobbying should be - and often is- a force for good, there was q genuine issue of concern that there is an inside track, who wields privileged access and disproportionate influence'. Amongst the report's conclusions was the recognition that some of the concerns that exist around improper influence are closely linked to the power of informal networks of friendship and relationships. Even though David Cameron 'predicted the lobbying scandal that now engulfs him', six years on from the 2008 report, Leveson appears to be showing us that not much has changed.

If lobbying is still a dirty word, can politics clean it up?

Leyer (1986) views the role of those involved in public affairs as 'the management of strategic issues : the approach to situations which constitute either an opportunity for the company, or a threat to it and which are connected with social and political changes, the formation of public opinion and political decision-making. Public affairs is more than trying to wield influence over Westminster. It is a holistic and strategic approach to communication and relationship building with a variety of governmental and non-governmental stakeholder groups. Of course, it is also about influence, but that's not new for any organisation. Lobbying behind closed doors may have given influence a bad name but we shouldn't shy away from it. Public affairs (as an activity) is taking over from lobbying, becoming more professional and honest. 'Organisations can no longer simply rely on 'who they know', the quality of their arguments is fundamental' (Thomson & John, 2007).

Van Riel & Fombrun (2007) suggest a number of best practices that government relationship specialists should apply and the skills they need, as shown in figure 1.

The Senior Examiner made the following comments.

'This extract demonstrates several strong features. First, the candidate signals that they understand the concept of public affairs and has drawn on a number of different sources in forming their argument. Second, the candidate offers some critical insight, not merely describing public affairs but attempting to comment on its practices as well. Third, the candidate supports their arguments with references and examples/evidence and relates these to their organisational sector. However the candidate will also have lost valuable marks here because references are not in the Harvard style. Fourth, the candidate uses current affairs and topical examples and so brings the debate right up to date. Finally, although not included here, the candidate then moves on to consider the role of public affairs within higher educational institutions and makes the case for its growing importance and relevance there'.

Other sample excerpts are freely available in the Senior Examiner Reports on the CIM Learning Zone website.

6 More Real World examples and updates

THE REAL WORLD

Public 'hysteria' over the role of the BBC

A year after the death of TV personality, Jimmy Savile, the accusations of inappropriate conduct with young children do not stop.

Many speak of a climate of tolerance at the BBC, where Savile worked on high-profile shows like *Top of the Pops* and *Jim'll Fix it*, with guests like the discredited pop star Gary Glitter.

It is as though executives and others turned a 'blind eye' to what may have been seen then as mere celebrity eccentric behaviour. Whether this is true, or not, remains to be seen, as momentum gathers for a full-scale investigation that promises to 'wash plenty of dirty laundry in public'.

Meanwhile, Sir Michael Lyons, Chairman of the BBC Trust from 2007 to 2011 was reported by The Sun as saying: 'There is a degree of hysteria in the extent to which (the scandal) is focused exclusively on the BBC. What we hear are not just allegations relating to the BBC, but also allegations made about hospital and prison contexts'.

The BBC is a publicly-funded organisation that has enjoyed a reputation over the years for 'doing the right thing'. At the time of writing (October 2012), the Savile scandal has the potential to damage this reputation greatly.

THE REAL WORLD

'Plebgate'

These days – and way back to Richard Nixon's time in office – any potential stain on an organisation's reputation, or that of a person, is called a 'something-gate'.

Andrew Mitchell, the Conservative Party Chief Whip got himself into the centre of a storm over a single incident when police apparently barred his way into Downing Street, on his bicycle. By police accounts, he swore at the officer(s), and mentioned the derogatory term 'plebs' (plebeian, or non-aristocratic person). It is for this latter, not the swearing that he got pillories. At the time of writing it appears certain that he will have to resign.

'He is not a credible figure', The Telegraph reported an MP as saying: 'He is doing so much reputational damage to the party and to David Cameron'. Thus, a single irate outburst, plus the fact that Andrew Mitchell seemed reluctant to clarify the issue, have cast a cloud over a senior statesman. How are the mighty fallen!

The Chartered Institute of Marketing

The change from traditional to digital: how a cycle shop gained global reputation

After 80 years, Butler's Cycles, a small independent cycle shop in Portsmouth took the plunge and embraced the Internet and digital trading. Re-launched in 1999 as http://www.wiggle.co.uk, the company began targeting active sports enthusiasts all over the world, with brands such as dhb, Verenti and Focus Bikes.

Thirteen years later, in 2012, their product range has expanded to over 250,000 products and a 45,000 sq foot warehouse, with deliveries to 70 countries. Wiggle is now considered the nation's number one online shop for cycles and accessories and the UK's fifth most popular online sports shop. Wiggle has won many awards for their service, including *220 Triathlon* magazine's 'Online Retailer of the Year' award for the previous four consecutive years, also coming top of a poll from consumer group *Which?* being voted 'UK's Top Sports & Leisure Shop'.

This success is very much in line with Government policy. In July, 2012, David Cameron has been quoted as saying that 'Britain is already now exporting more goods to the rest of the world than we are to the European Union: If we could increase the number of SME firms that sell overseas from one fifth to one quarter that would add £30billion to our economy, create 100,000 jobs and pretty much wipe out our trade deficit altogether.'

Wiggle sums up the secret of their success in the following: 'We have always believed in being the kind of company that we'd want to deal with if we were you. You have our absolute commitment as fellow active sports enthusiasts, Internet users and hardworking people that you'll be satisfied with Wiggle. Because the majority of people that work at Wiggle are "bike nuts" this is reflected through our passionate service and attention to detail. Nowhere else is this clearer than with our exclusive brands and products. With Brands such as we deal directly with the manufacturers shaping and tweaking the features and specification ensuring that the product you buy, is exactly what a true sports enthusiast would want.

Our expertise lies in offering incredible deals on a superb range of top quality mountain bikes, road bikes, bike parts and cycle accessories to buy, available with free delivery or our same day priority dispatch'.

A *Word Cloud* produced by Wiggle, reveals the word 'Service', as the single feature most commented by Customers.

North Face brought down by low-flying geese

At the time of writing, no-one can be sure what effect the scandal of the *foie gras* will have on the company's financial results. Only time will tell!

In the event, the company reacted very quickly to the reputational damage. Even while some newspapers were running the story, Joe Vernachio, North Face VP-Operations, was addressing the issue on the company blog, admitting that there was no short-term solution to the problem. He explained that grey geese are reared for their meat and especially for their liver and that whether the down (the neck feathers) were used or not, the process would continue. Under the heading 'Where we go from here', he said 'We believe we have an obligation to ourselves and our customers to better understand the source of materials in our supply chain and to advocate for the humane and ethical treatment of animals that are part of it and are committed to doing so. In addition we will seek a long-term solution that avoids sourcing down that is a by-product of force-feeding'.

A month later, the company blog is now announcing a new initiative: an *Animal-derived Materials Code of Ethics* that requires their supplier Allied Feather & Down to adhere to and implement with the suppliers and farmers in their supply chain. It said: 'North Face is committed to our goal of completely eliminating down, sourced from force-fed geese in our products by 2014'. Too little, too late? The company report of 2013 will tell the tale: will the bottom-line be down?

Virgin Rocks, OK!

Northern Rock had already introduced new corporate identity as far back as 2000 that, strangely enough, looks close to something from the Virgin Group.

A magenta square carried the Northern Rock logo, replacing the previous NR 'blocks' logo. Later in 2003, The Northern Rock Foundation also changed its logo, using the same new typeface. Northern rock used the design agency The Red Box Design Group, which designed the look of the buildings at the company's headquarters in Gosforth, contributing to other aspects of the company design, including the styling in-branch.

Now, during 2012, the Northern Rock brand will be gradually phased out, whilst Virgin Money – previously a solely online operation – has changed its corporate colours to embrace both the red of Virgin and Northern Rock's magenta. Clearly, the re-branding of Northern Rock is in its infancy and much more will have to be achieved in order to convince customers of its stability and integrity, two factors quite essential for a retail financial organisation.

Appendices

Appendix 1

A brief guide to Harvard referencing

1 A reminder regarding Harvard referencing

Harvard referencing is the preferred method of the CIM for you to state clearly the materials you use to complete your written assessments. Referencing serves two purposes. Firstly, it enables readers of your work to find the source documents for themselves and to read further into the topic, secondly, it avoids the problems of plagiarism (it is more difficult for you to be accused of copying another's work and passing it off as your own, if you have outwardly acknowledged their contribution).

Sometimes, Harvard referencing is referred to as the 'Author, Date' method. Although it is the most commonly used and highly structured method, you will find that there are slight variations amongst guides about the exact way to state references. For example, some suggest book titles should be written in italics whilst others state that they should be underlined. Whichever convention you choose is fine so long as you stick to the same throughout.

1.1 When and how do you reference within your paragraph?

Any time that you refer to the writing of another, their thoughts, theories, drawings or sayings, you should clearly cite their work. In practice, this means that there are two instances when you should state your reference. The first is within the paragraph where you are referring to their work and the second is at the end of your document, where you should provide a list of references.

To demonstrate how you cite a source within the paragraph you can consider the following example. It is likely that at some point in your CIM studies that you will want to refer to the work of marketing guru Philip Kotler. You may find yourself writing something similar to:

Kotler (1994) outlined that the process of marketing involves stages of analysis, planning, implementation and control

There are a few things to note from this:

1   The author Philip Kotler's name is used as part of the sentence. This means that his name (Kotler) is used and is then followed by the year of publication (1994) which is shown in brackets.

2   If there were two authors then you would write Kotler and 'Everyman' (year).

3   If there were more than two authors, then you would only use the surname of the first and refer to all others as *et al*. For example in this case if Kotler had co-authors then you would write Kotler *et al.* (1994).

If it did not seem appropriate to use the author's name within the sentence, you should still refer to them at the end of the sentence, for example you might have written:

The marketing process involves four essential stages: analysis, planning, implementation and control (Kotler, 1994).

Here you will see that before the final sentence full stop, you should have included in brackets the author's surname followed by a comma and then the year. There may be occasions that you find the same point is raised within more than one source. For example, you will be hard pressed to find a marketing textbook that doesn't identify one of the key roles of marketing as identifying and meeting customer needs. Rather than trying to identify which is the most appropriate to use you should use as many as is necessary. For example, you may write:

Marketing should encompass the notion that there is a need to identify and satisfy customer needs (Blythe, 2007; Hill and O'Sullivan, 2004; Kotler, 1994).

You should notice that the order of the sources is alphabetical according to author surname and that they are separated by a semi colon.

If you take a **direct quote** from the author, it should be referenced as follows: *'Marketing means working with markets to actualise potential exchanges for the purpose of satisfying human needs and wants'* (Kotler, 1994 **p.12). Note the inclusion of the page number!**

Again, you should use the author's surname and date within brackets following the italicised quote, but as it is a direct quote then you should provide more information to enable to reader to find it, by including a page reference.

Now that you have cited the source at the point that you refer to it, you should remember to add the entry to your reference list placed at the end of your document.

1.2 How do you cite different types of material within a reference list?

At the point within the sentence/paragraph where you cite your source, you will always use the author's surname and date regardless of whether the source was a book, newspaper or website. When you come to compile your reference list however, the nature of the material will determine how you structure your reference.

Examples of a number of types of materials are shown below along with examples of the convention being put into practice. As the convention is summarised, make sure that you pay attention to the use of underlining, italics, bold and grammatical marks.

Books

Author surname, Initial. (Year) *Book title*. Edition if more than one. City, Publisher.

Kotler, P. (1994) *Marketing Management: Analysis, Planning, Implementation and Control.* 8th edition. New Jersey, Prentice Hall.

Blythe, J. (2006*) Principles and Practice of Marketing.* London, Thompson.

Hill, L. and O'Sullivan, T. (2004) *Foundation Marketing.* 3rd edition. Oxford, Prentice Hall.

Edited books

Editor surname, Initials (ed) (Year) *Book title*. Edition if more than one. City, Publisher.

Bateson, J. E. G. (ed) (1991) *Managing Services Marketing: Text and Readings.* 2nd edition. Orlando, The Dryden Press.

Chapters or readings in a book

Author surname, Initials (Year) Chapter, reading, article title, in Editor surname, initial (ed), *Book title*. Edition if more than one, City, Publisher, pages.

Chase, RB (1991), Where does the customer fit in a service operation? in Bateson, J.E.G. (ed), *Managing Services Marketing*: Text and Readings. 2nd edition. Orlando, The Dryden Press, pp171-177.

Newspapers or magazines

Author surname, Initials or Anon (Year) Article title, *Journal or Newspaper*, Date.

Cowlett, M. (2007), PR Leagues, *Marketing*, 23rd May 2007.

Academic journals

Author surname, Initials (Year) Article title. *Journal*, Volume (Issue or Special Edition), pages.

Websites

Author, Initials (Year) Title Company/website owner details, web address [Accessed date].

Boots Group Plc., (2003) Corporate social responsibility, Boots Group Plc, http://www.Boots-Plc.Com/Information/Info.Asp?Level1id=447&Level 2id=0 [Accessed 23 July 2012].

Blogs

Author, Initials (Year) Title of document or page, [Online blog], website address [Accessed date].

Jay, S. (2008) Good affiliates are just ahead of the curve [Online blog], http://www.thedigitalmarketingblog.co.uk/2008/02/index.html [Accessed 12 March 2012].

Recorded broadcasts

Author, Initials (Year) Title of document or page [type of medium], Locating details [Accessed date].

Anon (2007) The Edwardian Larder [Television programme] BBC 4, [First Aired Monday 11 June 2007, 10.50pm-11.50pm].

Annual reports

Corporate author (Year) Full title of annual report. Place of Publication, Publisher.

Advertising Standards Authority (2006) ASA Annual Report. London, Advertising Standards Authority.

All references should be placed in alphabetical order. If you are referring to more than one source written by the same author, references should be listed in chronological order (earliest first).

1.3 How to work practically with Harvard referencing

There are software packages available such as Endnote, which can be used to file, sort, organise, insert within your text and automate your final reference list. Microsoft Word 2007 also now has referencing functionality, which will do the same. Although these packages will make referencing appear easier, the size of documents you will be working on probably would not warrant the investment. With this said, you will need to become highly organised as you read and start to make citations.

A tip worth trying:

Create a separate master document in which you complete the full reference list style citation in table format as shown below, as you refer to the source.

Table A   References: master document

Author/Year	Reference
Kotler (1994)	*Marketing Management: Analysis, Planning, Implementation and Control.* 8th edition. New Jersey, Prentice Hall.
Hill, L and O'Sullivan, T. (2004)	*Foundation Marketing.* 3rd edition. Oxford, Prentice Hall.
Anon (2007)	The Edwardian Larder [Television programme] BBC 4, [First Aired Monday 11 June 10.50pm-11.50pm].
Jay, S. (2008)	Good affiliates are just ahead of the curve [Online blog], http://www.thedigitalmarketingblog.co.uk/2008/02/index.html [Accessed 12 March 2012].

Open a blank table in a separate document, which you call *References for question x* (the specific question you are working on). As you insert a citation into your work, copy and paste the reference from your master document.

When you have finished your answer, sort the table alphabetically, merge the cells, tweak any line breaks etc. and make sure that you clear the border lines from around and within the table. The reference list below was formatted this way.

References

Anon (2007) The Edwardian Larder [Television programme] BBC 4, [First Aired Monday 11 June 10.50pm-11.50pm].

Hill, L and O'Sullivan, T. (2004) *Foundation Marketing*. 3rd edition. Oxford, Prentice Hall.

Jay, S. (2008) Good affiliates are just ahead of the curve [Online blog]. Available at: http://www.thedigitalmarketingblog.co.uk/2008/02/index.html [Accessed12 March 2012].

Kotler (1994) *Marketing Management: Analysis, Planning, Implementation and Control*. 8th edition, New Jersey, Prentice Hall.

1.4 So what is the difference between a list of references and a bibliography?

A bibliography will include all items that you have read throughout your studies which have helped to shape your thinking to be able to answer a particular question. A reference list will include only those sources, which you **directly** cite.

A bibliography should be placed directly after a reference list. This is not as relevant to your work and so you may wish to use only a list of references.

Useful online guides to referencing

CIM produces its own guide to Harvard referencing, available to download from: http://www.cimlearningzone.co.uk/assessment/harvard-referencing

Appendix 2

Grade descriptors (linked to the Magic formula)

Pass Grades at the level of the Chartered Postgraduate Diploma (Level 7)

(Adapted from Senior Examiner Reports, March 2012).

At this higher level, the grading focus has moved toward the **Application and Evaluation** of relevant theory, models and techniques, so that the Examiner will be looking to attribute 75% of the mark, based on these. Refer also to the requirement of 'postgraduateness', previously mentioned in this book.

Grade A (70% plus)

This is the top grade that everyone should be striving to achieve. You are required to be able to:

Presentation (10%)

- Engage confidently in academic and professional communication, reporting on actions clearly, autonomously and competently.

Concept (15%)

- Identify relevant theoretical principles commensurate with the postgraduate level, critically applying and evaluating these within a senior marketing management context, using originality of thought.

Application (30%)

- Critically analyse complex, incomplete or contradictory areas of knowledge of a strategic nature and communicate the outcome effectively.

- Synthesise information with critical awareness in a manner that is innovative and original.

- Utilise knowledge, theories and concepts from the forefront of the discipline/practice, demonstrating a mature and analytical understanding and awareness of managing and working at a strategic level.

Evaluation (45%)

Produce reliable valid and incisive conclusions and strategic recommendations based on findings.

Critically evaluate marketing concepts, theories and methodologies, arguing alternative approaches with evidence of an exceptional level of conceptual understanding of strategic issues.

Apply initiative and originality of thought in problem-solving, and decision-making in complex and unpredictable situations.

Grade B (60-69%)

Getting above 60% will take you into the B grade bracket, a really good pass. This grade is given for work that meets all of the assessment criteria and demonstrates a candidate's ability to:

Presentation (10%)

- Engage in academic and professional communication, reporting clearly, autonomously and competently.

Concept (15%)

- Identify relevant theoretical principles, commensurate with postgraduate levels, critically applying and evaluating these within a senior marketing management context.

Application (30%)

- Analyse complex, incomplete or contradictory areas of knowledge of strategic nature and communicate the outcome appropriately.

- Synthesise information in an effective manner, utilising appropriate knowledge, theories and concepts.

- Apply relevant contemporary issues, demonstrating a detailed understanding and awareness of managing and working at a strategic level.

Evaluation (45%)

- Produce reliable and informative conclusions and strategic recommendations based on findings. Evaluate marketing concepts, theories and methodologies, arguing a range of approaches, with evidence of a high level of conceptual understanding of strategic issues.

- Apply initiative in problem-solving and decision-making.

Grade C (50-59%)

You need to secure at least 50% for a pass. This grade is given for work that meets enough of the assessment criteria, demonstrating the following:

Presentation (10% of the mark, according to the Magic formula)

- To be able to engage in academic and professional communication, reporting clearly, autonomously and competently.

Concept (15%)

- To be able to identify relevant theoretical principles commensurate with postgraduate level and apply these within a senior marketing management context.

Application (30%)

- To be able to analyse areas of knowledge of a strategic nature and communicate the outcome satisfactorily. To be able to analyse information, in an appropriate manner, utilising knowledge of theories and concepts, including some contemporary issues.

- To be able to demonstrate an awareness of the context of managing and working at a strategic level.

Evaluation (45%)

- To be able to produce reliable conclusions and strategic recommendations based on findings.

- To be able to evaluate marketing concepts, theories and methodologies with evidence of a competent level of understanding of strategic issues.

- To be able to apply techniques of problem-solving and decision-making.

Grade D (45-49%)

This grade is given for borderline work that does not meet enough of the assessment criteria to secure a pass. This may be due to:

Presentation (10%)

Inappropriate use of academic and professional communication.

Concept (15%)

- Merely repeating case material, rather than evidencing knowledge of the marketing discipline at postgraduate diploma level.

Application (30%)

- A lack of knowledge and understanding of a strategic nature.

- Limited analysis of information, with limited reference to theories and concepts.

- Limited inclusion of contemporary issues and limited awareness or understanding of managing and working at a strategic level.

Evaluation (45%)

- Superficial conclusions and strategic recommendations, which lack depth.

- Insufficient evaluation of marketing concepts, theories and methodologies evidencing a lack of understanding of strategic issues.

- An inability to apply appropriate techniques for problem-solving and decision-making.

Appendix 3

Guidance on formats for CIM assessments

1   **Reports.** When producing a report. The candidate should adopt a formal style of writing in the third person. The document needs to be well structured, accurate, concise and clear. The following format provides one suggested approach for compiling the report, although an alternative approach is acceptable, if it results in a systematic well-organised document.

- Title page
- Terms of reference
- Procedure
- Executive summary
- Findings
- Conclusion
- Recommendations

2   **Discussion papers.** A discussion paper is a document created as a basis for discussion rather than as an authoritative statement or report will stop. It can take different forms. However, the following example illustrates possible approaches.

Example 1:

- Clear succinct title
- Name of author and date
- Terms of reference
- Abstract (short explanation or motive methods key results and conclusions)
- Introduction (motive of undertaking research
- Statement of the main findings
- Explanation/implication of the findings
- Alternative approaches
- Implications of alternative approaches
- Summary
- Recommendations
- Bibliography
- References

3   **Briefing papers.** A briefing paper includes relevant information about an analysis of a particular subject. The following example is in one possible format.

- Clear succinct title.

- Name of author and date

- Subject matter

- Background information

- Analysis

- Summary

- Recommendations

- Bibliography

- References

4   **White Papers.** A White Paper is a reference document that explores research arguments or schools of thought on a specific issue. The White Paper usually identifies the problem proposes solutions and looks at the benefits. It should also include a plan of action. A useful reference source is Michael Stelzner and *How to write a White Paper-a White Paper on White papers*. One possible approach is the following:

- Clear succinct title

- Name of author and date

- Subject matter

- Outline of problem. Issue four/area for investigation

- Evaluate the context, forward/background to the problem

- Propose solutions to resolve the problem including the benefits derived

- Propose a course of action

- Bibliography

- References

5   **Articles.** Articles are designed to appeal to a wider audience and therefore a balance needs to be achieved in producing a document that is both interesting to the reader, as well as being academically robust and appropriately referenced.

A suggested structure is shown below:

- Title

- Summary

- Introduction

- Body, with supporting facts

- Ending/closing

The Chartered
Institute of Marketing

The Chartered
Institute of Marketing

Review form

Please help us to ensure that the CIM learning materials we produce remain as accurate and user-friendly as possible. We cannot promise to answer every submission we receive, but we do promise that it will be read and taken into account when we update this Assessment Workbook.

Name: _____   **Address:** _____

_____

_____

1. How have you used this Assessment Workbook?
(Tick one box only)

☐ Self study (book only)

☐ On a course: college_____

☐ Other _____

3. Why did you decide to purchase this Assessment Workbook?
(Tick one box only)

☐ Have used companion Study Text

☐ Have used BPP Assessment Workbooks in the past

☐ Recommendation by friend/colleague

☐ Recommendation by a lecturer at college

☐ Saw advertising in journals

☐ Saw information on BPP website

2. During the past six months do you recall seeing/receiving any of the following?
(Tick as many boxes as are relevant)

☐ Our advertisement in *The Marketer*

☐ Our brochure with a letter through the post

☐ Our website www.bpp.com

4. Which (if any) aspects of our advertising do you find useful?
(Tick as many boxes as are relevant)

☐ Prices and publication dates of new editions

☐ Information on product content

☐ Facility to order books off-the-page

☐ None of the above

5. Have you used the companion Study Text?   Yes ☐   No ☐

6. Have you used the companion Passcards?   Yes ☐   No ☐

7. Your ratings, comments and suggestions would be appreciated on the following areas.

	Very useful	Useful	Not useful
Introductory section (Aim of the Assessment Workbook, etc)	☐	☐	☐
Chapter introduction: Unit overview and syllabus	☐	☐	☐
Syllabus learning outcomes	☐	☐	☐
Assessment tips	☐	☐	☐
Examiner's guidelines	☐	☐	☐
Structure and presentation	☐	☐	☐

	Excellent	Good	Adequate	Poor
Overall opinion of this Assessment Workbook	☐	☐	☐	☐

8. Do you intend to continue using BPP CIM products?   ☐ Yes   ☐ No

On the reverse of this page is space for you to write your comments about our Assessment Workbook. We welcome your feedback.

Please return to: CIM Publishing Manager, BPP Learning Media, FREEPOST, London, W12 8BR.

TELL US WHAT YOU THINK

Please note any further comments and suggestions/errors below. For example, was the text accurate, readable, concise, user-friendly and comprehensive?